Financial Survival Guide for Uncertain Times

Darnell .Y Glover

All rights reserved. Copyright © 2023 Darnell .Y Glover

Funny helpful tips:

Practice good posture; it reduces strain on the spine and enhances overall body function.

Practice contentment; it's the key to inner peace.

Financial Survival Guide for Uncertain Times : Navigating the Turbulent Tides: A Comprehensive Financial Strategy to Thrive in an Unpredictable Economy

Life advices:

Prioritize a balanced diet; the nutrients you consume play a pivotal role in determining your overall health and energy levels.

In the ocean of time, dive deep, exploring the depths of your potential.

Introduction

This is a comprehensive and insightful resource that equips readers with essential knowledge and practical strategies to navigate and prepare for various crisis scenarios. It provides an in-depth analysis of potential signs and indicators of economic collapse, drawing lessons from historical events like the Great Depression.

The guide emphasizes the significance of financial preparedness, offering advice on investing in precious metals, foreign currencies, cryptocurrencies, and other valuable assets. It also underscores the importance of developing useful skills and investing in tangible resources to ensure a secure and sustainable future.

Moreover, the guide delves into crucial aspects of crisis preparedness such as food acquisition and preservation, emphasizing the significance of stockpiling essential food items, growing food independently, and exploring hunting, trapping, and foraging as viable options. It also provides insights on preserving water and strategies to conserve this vital resource during challenging times. The guide goes on to discuss the significance of stockpiling equipment and supplies, gathering vital reference materials, and addressing primary survival concerns such as physical fitness, sanitation, cooking, warmth, lighting, alternative power, and security and defense.

With an emphasis on practical considerations, the guide addresses various additional factors, including handling crisis situations in apartments or condominiums, managing financial constraints during preparation, the importance of building relationships, and the art of adapting to a lifestyle with limited resources.

By encouraging readers to share knowledge and spread awareness, this book aims to foster a community that is well-informed, self-reliant, and equipped to navigate through potential crisis situations with resilience and preparedness.

Contents

What Does Collapse Look Like?..1
   Signs of Economic Collapse..2
   What Happens During Collapse?..4
   7 Lessons from the Great Depression..5
Prepare Yourself Financially..8
   What Can You Do to Prepare for Collapse?..8
   Should I Invest in Precious Metals?...10
   Are Foreign Dollars Worthwhile?..12
   What About Cryptocurrencies?...12
   Cash is King, to Some People...14
   Develop Useful Skills...16
   Invest in Real Hard Assets..17
   Final Thoughts on Preparing Financially...18
Food Acquisition and Preservation..19
   Stockpiling Food for Lean Times...19
   Growing Food for Hard Times...22
   Raising Food for Independence..23
   Hunting, Trapping, and Foraging...24
   Options to Preserve Food You Grow..25
   Final Thoughts on Food Acquisition..27
Water is Crucial to Survival..29
   How to Ration Your Most Precious Resource..30
   Final Thoughts on Water..32
Stockpile Equipment and Supplies..33
   11 Essentials That Are Hard to Make..33

- Where to Buy Survival Items Inexpensively 39
- Beyond Stockpiling Supplies 39
- Final Thoughts on Equipment to Stockpile 43
- Gather Vital Reference Materials 45
  - Entertainment for Boring Times 47
  - Final Thoughts on Reference Materials 49
- 7 Primary Survival Concerns 51
  - Physical Fitness and Health Problems 51
  - Sanitation and Hygiene 51
  - Cooking Food 52
  - Keeping Warm 54
  - Lighting Ideas 55
  - Alternative Power 56
  - Security and Defense 58
  - Final Thoughts on 7 Primary Survival Concerns 58
- 9 Additional Considerations 60
  - Children and Pets 60
  - Pest Control is Vital to Your Health 60
  - Why Bartering is a Bad Idea 61
  - Building Relationships is Essential 62
  - Learn to Do With Less or Without 64
  - Unnecessary Supplies and Actions 66
  - Living in an Apartment or Condominium 67
  - If You Cannot Financially Afford to Prepare 68
- Bringing Everything Together 70
- Get Your Free Checklist Here 74
  - Spread the Word, Share the Knowledge 74

What Does Collapse Look Like?

If you'd asked me a few years ago what America's collapse was going to look like, I would've said we're going to drown in a mountain of debt. How right—and possibly wrong—I'm proving to be. After all, who could've guessed that the past year and a half would include a worldwide pandemic, nationwide riots, and an ever-growing political divide that I'm afraid we can no longer resolve peacefully? I sure didn't, and I'm willing to bet you didn't either.

But then there's the nation's debt crisis, something that was bad to begin with and only getting worse after trillions upon trillions of COVID relief spending. Whether you believe it money well spent or not, one thing is for certain: At some point the bill from decades of massive spending will come due, and it will be you and I who end up paying the ultimate price through increased taxes, a higher cost of goods, and a slowing of economic growth which only serves to make the situation worse for those least able to afford it, including you and me.

I firmly believe we're headed for an economic catastrophe unlike any we've ever experienced; the only question is whether it will precede or succeed civil unrest, another pandemic, or even world war. I don't know the answer, but I believe the only solution Americans like you or me have is to prepare now, before it's too late.

Now, before I discuss how to do precisely that, let's talk about what an economic collapse might actually look like. Fortuitously or not, we have plenty of examples to draw upon throughout history, including the collapse of the Roman Empire during Diocletian, the French Revolution, the Russian Revolution, Spanish Bankruptcy in the sixteenth century, the Medici Bank failure in the late fifteenth century, as well as many others. Examples of hyperinflation, specifically, include Weimar Germany after World War I, Hungary in 1946, Argentina in 1998, and Zimbabwe starting in 2007. Both Greece and

Venezuela collapsed economically as recently as 2010, and they're both still feeling the effects of poor economic policies more than a decade later.

Unfortunately, poor money management by government officials is nothing new. The interesting part is that we've yet to see a complete global economic collapse, but that may come with the collapse of the U.S. dollar, as it's still considered the world's reserve currency. That said, China is doing their best to position the Chinese Yuan as the world's currency alternative which could hasten our collapse.

Signs of Economic Collapse

According to a letter penned in 2019, there are five signs of looming economic collapse: growing government debt, rising consumer debt, interest rate uncertainty, a slowing global economy, and political turmoil. You can view the charts here, if you like.

Let's start with government debt. As of year-end 2020, the U.S. national debt stands at almost twenty-eight trillion dollars, nearly triple what it was a single decade ago and almost ten times what it was thirty years ago. Our national debt has only climbed higher in recent months, largely because of COVID relief spending. Put in terms most people can attempt to fathom, twenty-eight trillion dollars is equivalent to twenty-eight million million dollars. That's a lot of millions, and there's no way we can ever pay it back.

Consumer debt doesn't look any better either. Aside from a clear dip because of COVID in 2020, the consumer debt curve nearly mirrors the government debt curve year after year, albeit on a slightly smaller scale.

On a positive note, the discount interest was slashed to 0.25% back in early 2020, also because of COVID. Although there's currently no uncertainty regarding the discount interest rate into the foreseeable future because the Federal Reserve has indicated it will keep rates low for the next year or two, it's rarely a good thing to delay a long overdue market correction. We'll see how this plays out over that time frame.

A proxy for the global economy can be measured by the Baltic Dry Index, a measure of demand for dry goods via global shipping. After looking at the chart for the past two years, including the entirety of 2020 and half of 2021, I will tell you that, aside from a major decline during the first half of 2020 as one would expect, the demand for dry goods is increasing to even higher levels than in 2019, which you might suppose is a good sign.

The last sign of economic collapse is political turmoil. I don't know about you, but I'd say we haven't seen this much political strife in a lifetime, and I'm not only talking about here in the United States. As I write this, Russia is amassing troops along the Ukrainian border, China is posturing over Taiwan, and the Israeli-Palestinian conflict is rearing up again. None of this bodes well for staving off economic collapse at home.

Ultimately, I'd say we're firmly at three out of the five major signs of economic collapse being met—growing government debt, rising consumer debt, and political turmoil—with the other two signs highly questionable because interest rates are being held artificially low by the Federal Reserve when they shouldn't be and the rising demand for dry goods is likely only a result of a year of unprecedented global shutdown.

At some point, the Federal Reserve along with other central banks will have no choice but to raise interest rates to combat rising inflation, which is precisely what happened in 1980 when the federal funds rate reached a high of twenty percent to combat, you guessed it, double-digit inflation after President Nixon completely disengaged the U.S. dollar from the gold standard in 1973. It's happened before.

It can happen again. And it will be worse because we refuse to take our medicine.

What Happens During Collapse?

Everything you might expect to happen, including:

- **Widespread unemployment** because of massive layoffs and shuttered businesses amid a lack of demand for a majority of the useless consumer goods we purchase. Expect poverty and hunger to set in relatively quickly thereafter.
- **High bankruptcy rates** because most people live paycheck to paycheck and, when they get laid off, cannot afford their already overpriced mortgage. As a side benefit —and I mean this facetiously—expect the government to seize bank accounts or, at minimum, a portion of your assets if you own anything of value.
- **A massive spike in crime and theft**. If you thought 2020 was bad, you haven't seen anything yet. When people get desperate, they get violent. Give them a few weeks without their government-issued checks coupled with no food at the grocery store and it will be a *Mad Max* scenario in every major city and most suburbs.
- **Hyperinflation**. Money will continue to lose purchasing power with increasing speed as the government attempts —and fails—to fix things. So long as we continue down the path of trying to fix the U.S. dollar, we'll see increasing prices across the board, particularly with food and energy costs.
- **Social chaos**. We'll witness more than protests and riots during a collapse, and when the government tires of our pleas, they'll send in the National Guard and declare martial law. This might actually be a good thing to quell the chaos, but it will also mean severely limiting your

movement as well as your ability to acquire goods and services. It might even result in the confiscation of anything of value you own.

Is an Economic Collapse the Only Way We Fall?

Not at all. As I mentioned previously, any global war could set off a collapse. Initially, Americans will rally, but as the public tires of war and as prices continue to rise, all bets are off as to what the government and Federal Reserve will do.

We've also seen cyberattacks recently on our critical infrastructure, and it's possible, albeit unlikely, that we could be subject to other forms of assault, such as an EMP strike or dirty bomb attack.

Let's not forget about our current political divide and civil unrest which are both still at critical tipping points. Far be it for me to suggest how this plays out, but it wouldn't surprise me if we see some sort of split of our great country soon. That would assuredly spur an economic collapse and worse.

Last, another pandemic like what we endured in 2020—or even a major resurgence of COVID—would surely spell disaster for an already fragile monetary system. Can you imagine how stagnant our economy will become, not to mention how many more stimulus checks will be printed, if we have another yearlong global lockdown? I shudder to think about it.

Whatever scenario becomes the final breaking point, expect it happen relatively quickly.

7 Lessons from the Great Depression

Assuming things play out similarly to our last major case study, the Great Depression, then we have some idea of what to expect on an individual level besides widespread unemployment, high bankruptcy rates, massive crime waves, hyperinflation, and social chaos.

Following are several ways life changed during the Great Depression.

1. Eating Habits Changed

Although most people didn't starve since there was often food available, they may not have had the foods they expected to consume. For instance, people switched from butter to Crisco and from fresh milk to evaporated milk because they were less expensive. Of course, sometimes the situation became more dire, such as when they ate Depression soup, which was simply one-third ketchup and two-thirds boiling water, but that was a rarity.

2. People Made Do With What They Had

They rarely bought anything new unless there was no other choice. People understood how to repair equipment when it broke down, how to mend clothes when it got holes, and how to fix tools rather than buying new ones like most of us do these days. The supplies and equipment they owned was made to last, unlike what we have now.

3. They Stretched Their Food Budgets

People used cornstarch as a thickener for soups, stews, gravies, and pies; oatmeal was used similarly to stretch their hamburger meat. They also rationed meat, incorporated root vegetables, and kept meals simple, whenever possible.

4. People Used Supplies in Unusual Ways

They lined their shoes with cardboard when the soles wore thin, used old tires to patch shoe soles, and turned scraps of paper bags into writing paper. If there was a way to make use of something they had lying around, they did.

5. Everything Was Used to the Last Drop

People used mesh bags to squeeze every bit of soap out of the chunks left behind, candle scraps were collected and remelted to make new candles, and every bit of fabric that could be salvaged was repurposed to make new clothes or linens. Wasting anything of use was not an option. In fact, they saved an array of items for reuse later, including clothing, sheets, towels, paper, buttons, string, tires, jars, and even kitchen scraps. Those who grew up during the depression era were fond of saying, "Use it up, wear it out, and make it do, or do without."

6. Everyone Worked

Young children did menial work or repetitive chores. Older children watched younger children and performed more tedious tasks, like running errands, cleaning the house, and harvesting crops.

7. Neighbors Still Helped Each Other

We can't do it all on our own, know everything, or never expect to not need help. Learn to be neighborly and you'll reap the rewards by building a community that sticks together.

We live in a very different society and time than our ancestors did nearly one hundred years ago. At the time of the Great Depression, for instance, twenty-five percent of Americans lived on farms whereas less than two percent do today. Many Americans had victory gardens—small vegetable, fruit, and herb gardens—raised chickens or other livestock, and knew how to live without electricity, running water, and central heating and cooling. They knew how to can food, butcher livestock, and hunt. Worse, much of what we consume and use is no longer made here in the United States, including some food. Even most of our prescription medications are made abroad, namely in China. None of this bodes well for hundreds of millions of Americans making it through a calamity like nothing we've ever seen. It's time to prepare yourself and your family, and here's how.

Prepare Yourself Financially

If you believe the U.S. dollar is an excellent investment, you're mistaken. The Federal Reserve has devalued the dollar since 1913, and it's becoming less valuable with increasing speed. Now, while I'm certainly not here to give financial advice, I will say this: If you're heavily invested in U.S. dollars, then you're setting yourself up for financial disaster when we collapse.

If you haven't noticed, inflation is rearing its ugly head now more so than ever. This is largely because of the unrestrained digital printing of money, among other shenanigans, by the Federal Reserve over the past decade and a half and, more recently, unchecked COVID relief spending. In fact, inflation is outpacing the government's ability to hide it.

But we won't only be paying the price via higher taxes and an ever-increasing national debt. No, we will pay the ultimate price when the cost of goods significantly outpaces earnings. Put another way: The true cost of nonstop monetary printing will be hyperinflation and, therefore, the average American's inability to buy the goods and supplies they need to survive. At that point, America will collapse into a shadow of its former glory, and it will be up to people like you and me to rebuild it from the ashes.

What Can You Do to Prepare for Collapse?

Start with reducing unnecessary debt and frivolous purchases. While I'm sure Dave Ramsey has quite a few ideas, some obvious examples include:

- Don't purchase a new car when your old one works just fine;
- Avoid eating out regularly when you can eat at home or make a lunch to take to work;

- Reduce or cancel unnecessary monthly expenses, such as inflated cable bills, excessive smartphone plans, and superfluous entertainment subscription services;
- Reduce personal care services like haircuts, manicures or pedicures, and massages, though my wife would vehemently disagree with this suggestion;
- Change or cancel vacation plans;
- Avoid impulse buys, especially online (you know I'm talking about you, Amazon).

Understandably, you can go much further with reducing unnecessary expenses in several ways, including:

- Avoid purchasing extended warranties or service plans;
- Lower insurance premiums on vehicles and for home or renters policies;
- Never gamble;
- Don't purchase gourmet drinks, alcohol, or cigarettes;
- Drop club memberships of all sorts unless you're a gym rat or you expect the membership to save you money, such as with wholesale membership clubs like Costco.

I'm sure you get the idea, though you're probably wondering what the point of reducing your expenses is if the U.S. dollar is going to be worthless soon, anyway. Fair enough.

The point is to use your newfound money to purchase preparedness gear and supplies that you wouldn't otherwise purchase. I'm not merely talking about more food, batteries, or toothpaste, though it never hurts to stockpile more of the supplies you already use. Instead, I want you to specifically focus on purchasing:

- Large water containers and extra water filters;
- Food storage containers and sturdy cookware, especially cast iron pans and a Dutch oven;

- Gardening tools of all kinds;
- Cutting tools, like a bow saw and an axe;
- Solar power equipment, such as solar panels, deep-cycle batteries, and a charge controller;
- Additional clothing for harsh weather (e.g., snow gear, boots, rain gear) and sleeping bags;
- Lamps and lanterns with plenty of fuel and wicks, or LED lanterns with a stockpile of batteries;
- Firearms and ammunition;
- Anything related to hygiene and sanitation, such as a washboard and clothesline, buckets, plenty of soap, and so on;
- Additional over-the-counter medications and medical supplies.

When hyperinflation truly hits, hundreds of items like these will be in short supply or too costly for most Americans to purchase because they're the very same items that we'll all need in our day to day lives. And just like anything else where timing matters, if you're late to the party, then you're going to be the one stuck holding the bag. Invest in survival and preparedness gear now.

Should I Invest in Precious Metals?

Spend even a short amount of time in any online prepper forum and you will come across somebody who says that the only way to survive an economic collapse is to convert all of your assets into gold and silver. That's hardly accurate, though there is some truth in their belief that precious metals are a good option, but it's not why most people think.

Before Roosevelt removed the United States from the gold standard back in 1933, the average American understood the benefits that holding physical gold and silver afforded them. Specifically, using precious metals as currency ensured the value of their money held steady because there were only so many gold and silver coins that could be produced. In addition, our ancestors understood the intrinsic melt value inherent in all precious metals. Gold and silver have long been trusted mediums of exchange because they are recognizable by most people, verifiable as genuine, and not as easy to debase as fiat paper currency, though governments have debased coins many times in the past.

The problem with relying on precious metals as a means of currency during collapse is that, believe it or not, many people won't know the value of what you're offering them. So, even if you tell them that a quarter-ounce gold coin is worth so much, they may not believe you. What's worse is that most people will initially be reluctant to accept a *new* form of currency, even if it's obvious to you they should.

Of course, if you're desperate for fiat currency in the short term, it's possible to liquidate small gold and silver coins, though you'll probably regret doing so because all fiat currencies are inherently less valuable than precious metals.

At some point, I believe physical gold and silver coins will be useful during a prolonged collapse, but likely not for months or years down the road. My advice would be to have some coins on hand as a long-term store of wealth and to only use them as a medium of exchange once most people realize their true value again.

A few words of warning:

- Only purchase small denomination coins for barter; anything one ounce or less should suffice, though you will pay a premium for the smaller denominations.
- Try not to pay over 5-8% of the spot price—the typical premium—for the day.
- Never buy for historical, or numismatic, value since these coins are rarely ever worth the markup associated with them.

- Stay away from ETFs, proof coins, cold calls or commercials selling you gold and silver, as well as investments in gold or silver mines.
- Find local dealers and then shop around. Sometimes you can find good, reputable dealers online, but it's always nice to look a person in the eye when it comes to your hard-earned assets.

Are Foreign Dollars Worthwhile?

I can't speak to holding foreign currency as a practical option to the U.S. dollar during a collapse, but I do know some savvy investors and preppers use them as a potential safe-haven for this very purpose.

The problem I have with using any fiat currency is that there's nothing stopping its issuing government from simply printing more currency whenever it chooses to, which inevitably leads to inflation and, therefore, a decrease in your purchasing power.

Even if you can find a foreign currency that you believe is stable and valuable, whomever you offer it to may not even know what it is. You'll end up with the same problem as you did with offering gold and silver as a medium of exchange.

In fact, I doubt most people could even recognize more than a few foreign currencies, and I'm willing to bet that most of the ones they could recognize aren't worth investing in as alternatives to the U.S. dollar. But, if you insist, consider diversifying a small portion of your U.S. dollars into other major currencies like the euro, the Australian dollar, the Swiss franc, and the Chinese yuan. Odds are that at least one fiat currency will still hold value during a collapse of the United States. Regardless, I believe Voltaire said it best: "Fiat currencies always eventually return to their intrinsic value—zero."

What About Cryptocurrencies?

I won't crush your enthusiasm for Bitcoin just yet, as it is an intriguing alternative, but I will say that the crypto-craze is happening for a reason, and that's because the world is quickly losing faith in the U.S. dollar as a storage of wealth.

As I write this, Bitcoin's price has taken a dip under $40,000 USD, which makes me feel like it's on sale, but the only reason Bitcoin cost so much to begin with is because of the inflated U.S. dollar. Believe it or not, some say that Bitcoin will reach a million dollars within the next handful of years, though, in fairness, that's coming from people who have a vested interest in it doing so.

You might suppose it's a good thing if Bitcoin prices soar, but it's not. If cryptocurrency prices continue to skyrocket, what it really means is that the U.S. dollar is virtually worthless as a storage of value. On a positive note, if you invest in Bitcoin well before it reaches astronomical prices, then you will have largely preserved the purchasing power of the money you converted, which means you might still be capable of purchasing the goods and services you need to survive. Maybe.

The bad news is that you might never get to use your Bitcoin because the government won't allow it. But I thought cryptocurrencies were decentralized, you ask? They are, though it doesn't mean the powers that be won't take steps to limit or outright ban their use. In fact, nearly twenty countries have already limited or banned cryptocurrencies for one illegitimate reason or another.

In addition, once central banks like the Federal Reserve develop their own cryptocurrencies, I'm willing to bet that decentralized cryptocurrencies—including Bitcoin—will become illegal or severely restricted here in the United States, possibly worldwide. I'm also willing to bet that all major retailers will quickly fall in line with governmental demands, so you won't have a choice in the cryptocurrency you're allowed to use. Granted, it may still be possible to conduct individual transactions with like-minded individuals using decentralized cryptocurrencies, but it won't surprise me if using Bitcoins—or any cryptocurrency—becomes outright illegal as was using gold during the thirties.

Obviously, I don't know this for sure, so take what I say with a grain of salt. Regardless, I would be wary of jumping headfirst into the crypto-craze without at least considering the implications of future government actions.

What Cryptocurrency Should I Purchase?

Let me answer that question with one of my own: Can you even name a cryptocurrency besides Bitcoin? Most people probably cannot. If it were me, I would stick with the one currency everyone knows and is relatively familiar with—Bitcoin. This Investopedia article is a good read because it explains all about Bitcoin, including how Bitcoin works, why it has value, how and where to purchase Bitcoin, and plenty more.

If you want other suggestions, try Ethereum or possibly Litecoin. Stay away from gimmicks like Dogecoin or PotCoin—yes, it's literally intended for the cannabis industry—and anything being hyped online. Remember that the point of cryptocurrencies is to be a hedge against inevitable inflation, not a get-rich-quick scheme.

Cash is King, to Some People

I'm about to blow your mind. U.S. dollars will continue to be desired by some people until the bitter end. Until these people come to terms with the fact that what they're holding isn't worth the paper it's printed on, you will find people who will continue to accept—even demand—cash as their preferred form of payment throughout a collapse. Maybe these people have no other choice since they never invested in an alternative, who knows. Whatever the reason, it may be wise to hold a small portion of your assets in U.S. dollars, preferably held in hard cash at home. Money in your bank account doesn't count.

Reconsider Keeping Money in the Bank

One of the many problems with economic collapse is that governments often take drastic actions when things get completely out of hand, including confiscating bank accounts, personal property, and even homes. During the Cyprus bailout in 2013, for example, people heard that the government would seize up to ten percent of savings from bank accounts without warning, but they eventually chose to only seize banks accounts above one hundred thousand euro; how nice of them to spare the little guys.

When word gets out of confiscation efforts—or even if there's only a fear of it happening—the next predictable consequence is a run on the banks and an eventual bank holiday being declared. At that point, there will be no money to be had for a significant period.

So, if your bank account isn't the best place to store money, then what is? That's tough to answer because there isn't a perfect solution. Some suggest keeping stashes of money at home, such as in a safe or even under the mattress, but there's always the genuine concern of theft or fire. Perhaps a safe deposit box is a better option, though they have been pilfered and, to make matters worse, banks are not required to compensate customers if their property is damaged or stolen from a safe deposit box.

Are credit unions any better than traditional banks? Not really since they'll likely fall prey to confiscation efforts just like any traditional bank account would.

Ultimately, I'd say the best, safest option is to purchase a quality, heavy-duty, fireproof safe that's too bulky to move and, preferably, bolted down to the floor or wall. And if you can hide it from sight, then all the better, which means your bedroom closet is the worst place to hide valuables, even if they're stashed in a safe.

Develop Useful Skills

Perhaps the best hedge against inflation during a collapse is to possess skills that other people will find useful, especially those who can afford it because there will be people with needs and the money to pay for it. The best skills to develop are those that require a fair amount of training and expertise to do well, including:

- All medical professionals, such as doctors, pharmacists, nurses, dentists, paramedics, and veterinarians;
- Military or security guards and police officers;
- Skilled trade jobs, such as electricians, plumbers, welders, or HVAC technicians;
- Auto mechanics;
- Anyone with construction and building experience.

Surely, I wouldn't expect you to spend years developing one of the aforementioned skills for when society collapses, but if you're already a part of one of these professions, keep your skills up to date as you may be in high demand when times get tough. At the very least, you can pass down your knowledge to those eager and willing to learn, and likely even be paid handsomely for your time and knowledge.

If the skills you possess don't fall into one of the above categories, don't fret. There are easily dozens of talents that people will find useful during a collapse. For example, can you sew or knit? Clothes and linens will need mended, which means sewing skills will be in demand. Can you identify local flora and fauna? How about edible mushrooms and berries? Perhaps you know how to hunt or trap. Everyone needs to eat, and if traditional food is in short supply, your knowledge and skills may fill the gap. Or, maybe you fancy yourself a gunsmith, herbalist, or all-around handyperson. It doesn't much matter what you can do so long as you have a useful survival-related skill. Thus, any skill is excellent to know, and I'm sure someone will pay you for your knowledge and time if you're open to the possibility.

Invest in Real Hard Assets

Traditionally, hard assets are investments in real estate, precious metals which we've already covered, commodities like agricultural or forestry products, vehicles and machinery, as well as paintings and collectibles. Basically, a commodity is any physical asset that holds value, though not all hard assets are created equal regarding collapse survival.

Think about it, shouldn't a piece of farm machinery be more useful than a famous painting during a collapse? Or wouldn't a plot of trees be more valuable than a room full of antique clocks? Clearly, which is why it's important to invest in hard assets that should prove useful to you—and others—during a lengthy survival situation. This could include almost anything directly related to food production, tool manufacturing, heavy machinery, fuel and energy acquisition, natural resource production (e.g., trees), and medications.

I recognize that most of us cannot afford to invest in large tracts of farmland, heavy machinery, or solar farms for the coming collapse. We can, however, invest in our own forms of hard assets for personal use. Although we'll discuss several options later—including investing in books and gardening supplies—think about the tools and equipment that you might need to rely upon if you had to be far more self-reliant than you are now.

We've already mentioned several ideas earlier in the chapter, including large water containers, cookware, solar power equipment, lamps and lanterns, and firearms to name a handful of ideas. Now consider other tools and equipment that might prove useful during hard times, such as construction tools, hand tools, anything used around a homestead, outdoor stoves, a quality grain grinder, and so on. The sky is the limit with survival tools and equipment that could prove useful; we'll discuss the specifics to focus on in a later chapter.

Of course, I wouldn't expect you to go out and purchase everything you could possibly think of. That would get expensive, fast. Instead, gather equipment over time, scour yard sales for deals, and even consider working with family, friends, and neighbors to gather equipment that could be mutually beneficial, assuming you expect to attempt collapse survival with these people.

Final Thoughts on Preparing Financially

The main takeaways regarding your financial preparedness include:

1. Get out of U.S. dollars as much as possible.
2. Diversify to alternative currencies, including precious metals, foreign currencies, and cryptocurrencies.
3. Don't keep all your money in the bank. Keep some in the bank, a portion in a safe deposit box, and more at home in a quality, hidden fireproof safe.
4. Develop useful skills because bartering your knowledge and abilities will be about the only way for most of us to earn an income during a lengthy collapse.
5. Invest in real hard assets—such as homesteading tools and equipment—because they will be difficult to acquire, expensive, and worth their weight in gold after a collapse.

Food Acquisition and Preservation

We instinctively know that food is crucial to our survival, even though most of us don't act like it is. Why do I say that? Because most people do nothing to ensure they'll have enough food to eat should something—anything—happen which disrupts their ability to acquire more from the local grocery store anytime they like.

Sadly, I still know people who go to the store or eat out multiple times a week, and if you were to look in their refrigerator or pantry, you would be shocked at how little food they actually have on hand; the worst part is that some of these people I know have children. It's as if they're completely oblivious, ignorant, or both regarding how fragile our just-in-time manufacturing system truly is when there's a hiccup.

That said, food manufacturers and distributors did much better than I assumed they would during the 2020 pandemic, so my hats off to them for their efforts. Still, we haven't seen anything yet with just how scarce goods and supplies can become when people are desperate. As an idea of how bad things can get, take the worst of what you saw during the pandemic regarding shortages and multiply it by a hundred, and then expect nothing to get resolved for a year or longer. Granted, our situation may never truly get that bad, but we need to prepare like it will.

Stockpiling Food for Lean Times

With the above in mind, let's talk about stockpiling food to get you through the initial catastrophe because, no matter how much gold or Bitcoin you have stashed away, it's entirely possible that food—among other necessary supplies—simply won't be available at any reasonable price. I say this because when prices skyrocket, they often increase rapidly for everything in the supply chain. This includes the raw materials, labor, and transportation costs necessary to make and deliver consumer goods—in this case, the foods that you and I are so accustomed to expecting at our local grocery store.

Clearly, there will still be people trying to feed the desperate masses, à la the depression-era bread lines, but you don't want to be one of the unprepared people looking for a handout, do you? Of course you don't. Therefore, you'll want to focus on three major groups of food to gather:

1. Nutritious, shelf-stable foods that provide most of your vitamin and mineral needs;
2. Bulk foods that act as filler and provide calories;
3. What I call "superfoods" to supplement your nutritional intake.

Now, although I *wrote a book about 57 Scientifically-Proven Survival Foods to Stockpile*, if you'd like to read it, the easiest thing to do here is to reproduce an abridged checklist of foods to stockpile for ease of reference:

Grocery Store Foods to Stockpile

- Breakfast cereals
- Canned beans
- Canned chili
- Canned chowder
- Canned fish
- Canned fruits
- Canned meats
- Canned soups
- Canned vegetables
- Chocolates
- Cookies
- Cooking oils, lard, butter
- Ingredients to make bread
- Iced tea
- Jelly
- Mayonnaise
- Nuts and nut butters
- Pasta sauce
- Popcorn kernels
- Potato chips
- Pre-mixed canned drinks
- Pretzels
- Seasonings

- Crackers
- Hard candies
- Seeds
- Sweetened powdered drink mix

Bulk Foods to Stockpile

- Beans, assorted
- Berry drink mix
- Cocoa mix
- Granola
- Macaroni
- Nonfat dry milk
- Oats
- Pancake mix
- Potato flakes
- Spaghetti
- White rice

Superfoods to Stockpile

- Apple cider vinegar
- Cacao powder
- Chia seeds
- Chlorella
- Coconut oil
- Digestive enzymes
- Eggs
- Fiber powder or psyllium husk powder
- Fish oil or Omega-3
- Flax seeds
- Green tea
- Liquid minerals or multivitamin
- Multivitamin
- Probiotics or water kefir grains
- Protein powder
- Raw honey
- Spirulina
- Vitamin C powder
- Wheat germ

With the above list in hand, you'll be able to stockpile enough food to see you and your family through months of food shortages with little concern. Before we move on, I should mention that if your family won't eat a specific food I recommend, please don't purchase it as the food will only go to waste. Similarly, if there are shelf-stable foods you consume regularly, then I strongly encourage you to include plenty of them in your pantry because they will be expected and welcome. Last, if anyone in your family has a very specific dietary consideration, such as celiac disease, which prevents them from eating common foods, then do whatever you can to prepare for it now because specialty foods will be among the most difficult to acquire during hard times, particularly during the onset.

Growing Food for Hard Times

My father-in-law genuinely enjoys vegetable gardening; it's a passion of his. I, however, consider all forms of gardening tedious. Regardless, we both recognize how crucial planting and harvesting our own food will be during a collapse. Vegetable gardening may, in fact, be the difference between our survival and not. Realize, however, that it's not only about having food to eat but about having the right food to eat.

Whereas you and I can still easily purchase years' worth of bulk food—rice, dry beans, noodles—and have plenty to consume day in and day out, the same shelf-stable foods that most preppers love to stash will only stave off starvation. In fact, what bulk food cannot do is provide you with the nutrition that only comes from vegetables, fruits, meat, and dairy. Thus, taking steps to put back and acquire these specific nutritious foods is a must.

Most people begin by planting a vegetable garden, which, although hard work and sometimes frustrating, is one of the most reliable ways to procure your own nutrient-dense food. Start with easier vegetables to grow, such as carrots, potatoes, tomatoes, lettuce, green beans, and zucchini, and you'll have a green thumb before you know it. Then, as you gain confidence, move on to the more difficult vegetables to grow, like broccoli and cauliflower, if you dare.

In fact, consider specifically focusing on vegetables that you can regrow from scraps, such as potatoes, onions, celery, and carrots. I also recommend you learn to save seeds for the next planting season as well as learn how to can, dehydrate, or freeze-dry excess vegetables for lean winters.

Another great option for long-term survival is to plant fruit trees. Sadly, most fruit trees take several years to produce a harvest from seed, which isn't very helpful if you expect a collapse soon. Fortunately, if you get started now and we don't collapse for a handful of years, then you'll be in much better shape than having done nothing at all. To speed things up, I strongly recommend you purchase grafted fruit trees, which will shave years off harvest time. It's a simple decision if you ask me.

Realize, too, that some types of fruit trees produce faster than others. For instance, peach trees, apple trees, and citrus fruit trees grow relatively fast, though the species you choose does matter as some varieties produce faster than others, so you'll want to do your homework before purchasing just anything. In addition, be sure to check your hardiness zone and then determine which fruit trees are best suited to your climate so you don't end up with a dead tree.

Last, I would be remiss if I didn't mention fruit-bearing bushes and vines; blueberries, strawberries, raspberries, and grapes are all popular favorites among backyard growers. Plant them along fence lines and other less-used locations and you'll have a bountiful garden before you know it.

Raising Food for Independence

I'll admit, I'm not yet here on my preparedness journey. While I've long considered myself a prepper, I've yet to become a self-sufficient homesteader, which is something I intend on rectifying soon, God-willing. Thus, I can't speak from personal experience regarding animal husbandry or even raising chickens, although chickens will be first on my list. My wife insists. Why? Because eggs are one of the more nutritious foods you can consume, and since most chickens produce eggs throughout much of the year, you'll have a ready supply of fresh food that you'll soon tire of eating.

Other Animals to Raise

Chickens aren't the only animal to raise, far from it. Homesteaders often raise goats, cows, hogs, ducks, rabbits, and even insects, like bees. Some animals are better scavengers and self-sufficient if you let them roam, whereas others require more feeding and attention. Which you choose is up to you, but I wouldn't get overly ambitious right from the start. Begin with something small, like chickens or rabbits, and then move on to larger animals such as goats or pigs when you're ready. Yes, we're attempting to prepare for societal collapse, but that doesn't mean you should collapse from work and stress to make it happen.

A final food I want to mention is fish, namely tilapia, raised in either a pond or, more likely, an aquaponics tank. If done right, you'll have fish that will reproduce every month or two with very little effort or intervention on your part as well as another source of meat.

Hunting, Trapping, and Foraging

I'm not a hunter, and I don't trap or forage for food, but if you do or if you know somebody who does, that's a good thing because we may need to resort to more primitive means of gathering food again. Realize that hunting and trapping will require you to process whatever you come home with, which is something many hunters I know don't actually do themselves.

In addition, be aware that nearly everyone who is a hunter, trapper, or forager will be out doing the same thing as you are, so the game populations will dwindle quickly post-collapse and, worse, could become a dangerous means of food procurement when people get desperate and see you as a threat or impediment to feeding themselves and their families.

Options to Preserve Food You Grow

While buying food to stockpile is undoubtedly the easiest short-term solution, I recognize many people are quite concerned with the quality of the food they purchase. And if you expect the most nutritious foods to be less available during a collapse, it's wise to preserve your own. It will benefit you to learn to can, dehydrate, or even freeze-dry fruits and vegetables.

Whereas canning is labor intensive and cheap, freeze-drying is fairly easy but takes a special and expensive piece of equipment like the Harvest Right Freeze Dryer. Dehydrating falls somewhere in the middle regarding effort and expense. Without a doubt, freeze-drying food is better than canning and dehydrating—you really can't beat the results—though the upfront cost of a freeze-drying unit will dissuade all but the most ardent of preppers.

Another option is to purchase freeze-dried foods online but be prepared for sticker shock. When I used to sell Thrive Life foods, for example, a #10 can of diced chicken cost around $60 and was, admittedly, more expensive than most other freeze-dried options. And although I can't find a #10 can of diced chicken at Thrive Life any longer, after a quick look online I found that most #10 cans of diced chicken sell for between $80-100 per can with a few exceptions. That's just too much to pay for a single can of diced freeze-dried chicken if you ask me. If you're willing to pay the initial investment, I recommend an at-home freeze dryer as the best long-term option to store the most nutritious foods in the best possible manner.

If a freeze dryer is too expensive, take up dehydrating by purchasing an Excalibur Dehydrator, then spend some time reading

Dehydrate2Store.com; it's one of the best resources I've found about dehydrating.

If you insist on canning, you're going to want an excellent book on the topic, and I can't think of anything better than the *Ball Complete Book of Home Preserving*. You might also be interested in *A Guide to Canning, Freezing, Curing & Smoking Meat, Fish & Game* as it includes details on meat and fish preservation.

Root Cellars and Cold Storage

So now you've got a plan to grow and preserve an assortment of fruits and vegetables, maybe some meat and dairy as well. That's great, but what happens if the power grid is down, your solar power system is being used for something besides powering the refrigerator, or you have so much extra food that it can't all fit? Or, perhaps you can only power a small refrigerator and you need to save that space for your meats and dairy? In this case, I wholeheartedly encourage you to consider an in-ground root cellar or cold storage for most of your fruits and vegetables.

You don't need to build anything fancy. Try burying an old chest freezer or refrigerator or simply bury and cover a garbage can. Alternatively, you could build your own outdoor walk-in root cellar from scratch or simply wall off part of an underground basement like I did many years ago. So long as the cold storage area can be kept cool, humid, dark, and well-ventilated, you're in good shape.

Understand that a root cellar is only appropriate for some fruits and vegetables—like potatoes and apples—as well as some waxed cheeses but never for meats or dairy. Home-canned foods are great to store here as well, but you'll want to avoid including dehydrated or freeze-dried foods because of the high humidity levels unless you store them for the long-term using either canning jars with the oxygen removed using a Foodsaver or Mylar bags and oxygen absorbers, something you should do, anyway.

If the idea of a root cellar interests you, then I recommend you read *Root Cellaring* by Mike Bubel. It was the book that got me into building my root cellar over fifteen years ago, and it's still a great reference.

Bulk Food Storage

Any dry goods you intend to store for the long-term, such as rice, dry beans, noodles, and wheat, should be kept dry, cool, and away from sunlight. Avoid keeping any food in extremely hot locations like a non-air-conditioned garage, shed, or attic. Freezing temperatures aren't great either unless you're specifically freezing wheat, for instance, to kill off larvae before long-term storage.

It's best to keep bulk foods stored in a food grade bucket because it won't leech harmful chemicals. Alternatively, storing food in a Mylar bag with an oxygen absorber works great too if you intend to use just any five-gallon bucket with an airtight lid. There are other methods you can use, such as dry ice, but stick with the easiest methods and you'll be glad you did. Remember, too, that proper storage in sturdy buckets helps to control insects and rodents, though rats have been known to chew through plastic containers.

Final Thoughts on Food Acquisition

Planning how to feed your family for the coming lean times is crucial to begin now. Luckily, there are many possibilities available to you, and I would encourage you to attempt more than one. Remember that doing so will be difficult to accomplish after collapse when everyone else is trying to do the same thing, so you really need to get started soon.

At minimum, I suggest you stockpile enough shelf-stable foods to see you through a few months of uncertainty. If you can expand your stockpile to several months or longer, then that would be preferable. In addition, add more food year after year. Whether that's gardening, raising chickens or rabbits, hunting, foraging, or all of the above, get to it.

I have a few more thoughts I want to cover but which didn't fit nicely anywhere else. First, you need to be aware of a concern called appetite fatigue. Essentially, it occurs when a person tires of eating the same food repeatedly because it doesn't taste good to them. Appetite fatigue can get so bad that a person will stop eating even if they're starving; children are especially prone to this problem. Clearly, relying on bland beans and rice every night for dinner isn't a good plan. To combat appetite fatigue, it's vital that you store a wide variety of food to keep one's tastebuds engaged. Also, storing an assortment of spices and seasonings is another great way to liven up the same boring food.

Second, although you may feel you have enough food stored for you and your family at some point, there's a genuine possibility that you'll have additional—even unexpected—mouths to feed. Whether you choose to feed them is at your discretion, but you could choose to take in extended family members or friends specifically because they can be helpful to you during hard times. Even if you never intend to feed more than the number of mouths you planned for, it never hurts to have more food stashed away.

Third, I suggest you add some sort of multivitamin or supplements to your stockpile because, although I expect you to include nutritious foods in your survival strategy, it's entirely possible that, despite your best efforts, you'll still end up lacking an important nutrient in your diet. Luckily, you can address this problem with a quality multivitamin, most of which are shelf-stable and viable for years. It's easy to store a few years' worth of multivitamins without concern.

Water is Crucial to Survival

Even though water is arguably more crucial than food for your immediate survival, I'll assume that water procurement will continue to be easier than food procurement during a collapse. This won't be universally true for everyone, though most of us can figure out how to collect rainwater or haul water in buckets if it comes to that.

The problem becomes how to make water procurement sustainable and potable with minimal impact on your day because, believe it or not, there are still women who spend hours each day hauling water home for their families.

So, unless you intend to drill a well, which is a wonderful solution but can get expensive, the only other option for most of us is to collect rainwater. In order to make rainwater harvesting truly beneficial, you're going to want to use large storage containers. The traditional 55-gallon water barrels simply aren't large enough unless you have extremely limited space. I prefer IBC totes of 270 or 330 gallons, though there are much larger water tanks, called cisterns, if you want to go big. Simply search your local online ads as will be discussed shortly and then search YouTube for "IBC Tote Rainwater Collection" and you'll find plenty of videos to walk you through the setup, though this YouTube playlist is a good one to start with.

Once you have a rainwater collection system set up, you'll need to purify the water to make it safe to consume because there are plenty of debris, bacteria, and chemicals that will be picked up from your rooftop. Perhaps the easiest way to do so is with a quality gravity water filter. Personally, I've used a Berkey Water Filter System for several years and love it. Yes, it is an expensive initial investment, and you will want to purchase additional Black Berkey Purification Elements, but it's well worth the outlay as a dependable, off-grid water treatment option.

Aside from the larger water containers and gravity filters, you're going to want some buckets to haul water from your water containers to the Berkey system. Although food grade buckets are preferable, any clean five-gallon bucket should suffice.

Last, while not because it's inherently unsafe, some state authorities have banned rainwater harvesting to some degree or another. Fortunately, it's usually easy to comply with their regulations. That said, do everything you can to treat and purify all collected water from any source because, even if it looks clean, water can harbor many nasty pathogens you don't want to consume.

How to Ration Your Most Precious Resource

Aside from breathing clean air, water is arguably the most precious resource we take for granted. Remarkably, the average American uses upwards of one hundred gallons of water each day for indoor use, primarily to flush toilets and bathe. There's no way you and I can continue to consume that much water post-collapse; rationing water is a must.

Human consumption and personal hygiene are the two most important uses of water, a precious resource. Thus, most of any stored water you have must be labeled for these purposes alone.

Given that the typical adult could consume a gallon of water per day, use another gallon or two for cooking, and need a few gallons for personal hygiene—including brushing your teeth, washing your hands, and minimal bathing—I suggest you plan on five gallons of water per person per day as the bare minimum to store. Depending on where you live, it could go weeks or longer without raining, so you need to plan for that likelihood. If it were to go a month without raining, for example, that means you'd need to store approximately 150 gallons of water per person at minimum; a family of four would require 600 gallons of water to see them through. This equates to roughly eleven 55-gallon barrels or only two IBC totes of water.

Obviously, five gallons of water per day is a far cry less than the one hundred gallons most of us use daily. So, what gives? Flushing toilets is big. You'll be digging holes and using makeshift chamber pots at night. And if you can dig a large enough hole for an outhouse, then all the better. While I'm not saying there will be no functioning toilets during a collapse, water, like food, may become much more costly to afford, so collecting rainwater and rationing is always a good idea.

Bathing is another big water waster. Learn to bathe with far less water, specifically by using a sponge or washcloth and only turning on the water to wet yourself down initially and then to rinse off when you're done. Some people call this a military or Navy shower.

Aside from not flushing toilets and reducing water used while bathing, there are other ways to conserve water, particularly by using the three-pot method to wash dishes. Basically, you take three buckets or bins and fill the first with a solution of hot soapy water, the second with only warm water for rinsing, and the third with a bleach solution of two teaspoons of bleach to one gallon of cold water as a disinfectant. Let air dry.

Washing clothing is the final major use of water indoors. Regrettably, washing clothes by hand in tubs of hot water with a washboard and scrub brush is a tedious process and a major reason why pioneers only washed clothes once a week, typically on Monday, their "wash day." To reduce your wash load, set aside clothing specifically for outdoor use only and wash your indoor clothing sparingly.

Domesticated pets need water, too, though not nearly as much as humans. And if you have a vegetable garden or farm animals which may require copious amounts of water, then I would suggest a dedicated water supply for them so that, if things get dire enough, you're not carelessly using water needed for human consumption on farm animals or even a garden. Let nature take care of natural things while you focus on yourself and your family's needs.

Final Thoughts on Water

Having a reliable source of water is as important as food, if not more so. If you're homesteading and can drill a well, then do it. If that's not workable—and even if it is—then collect rainwater. Use as large of containers as you can and then be sure you have plenty of gravity filters to treat what you collect.

Keep at least a few hundred gallons of water on hand (five gallons per person per day) at all times for drought conditions, and if you live somewhere that you know it rarely rains, then store much more.

Last, ration the water you collect as much as possible without sacrificing your health. Focus on human consumption and cooking, personal hygiene, dishes, laundry, pets, and then all other uses, in that order.

Stockpile Equipment and Supplies

There's so much you can purchase for collapse survival that it can feel overwhelming. With that in mind, we'll start with eleven essential items most people would have a hard time replicating or doing without during a collapse scenario. After that, we'll discuss where to purchase supplies inexpensively as well as how to go about making your own homemade personal hygiene supplies, household cleaners, and more using only a handful of ingredients for when times get really tough.

11 Essentials That Are Hard to Make

If there are any supplies to focus your initial attention and money on, it's these.

1. Over-the-Counter Medications

Whereas prescription medications are a problem because you simply cannot purchase years' worth of them at one time, over-the-counter medications can be readily obtained at dirt-cheap costs relative to their usefulness in a post-collapse world. I suggest you purchase plenty of analgesics, decongestants, antihistamines, antacids, antidiarrheals, and even laxatives. Add in an assortment of topical analgesics, topical steroids, and antibiotic ointment and you'll have most of your first aid bases covered.

Luckily, many over-the-counter medications will [last much longer than their expiration date]. There are exceptions, such as with some liquid medications, as well as potential storage concerns, like being subject to extreme heat or humidity, but if you store your OTC medications in climate-controlled conditions, then they'll last much longer. As was the case with long-term food storage, heat, humidity, oxygen, and light are the biggest factors that degrade most shelf-stable medications.

Should you stockpile antibiotics? If you're unable to get proper medical care, then fish antibiotics might be a last resort. I will point out, however, that fish antibiotics are not approved by the FDA for human consumption, and you might actually cause more harm than good if you're dealing with a viral infection or using the wrong antibiotic. It's also illegal to import traditional antibiotics from overseas or to purchase them online without a doctor's prescription. My advice: Don't take chances with your health, even during a collapse; seek proper medical advice.

2. Glasses, Contacts, and Hearing Aids

Our five senses are something most of us take for granted, at least until they no longer work properly and then they become absolutely precious. The ability to see and hear, in particular, is vital during emergency situations and will be equally important during a collapse.

If you already rely on glasses, contacts, hearing aids, or dentures, then I recommend you have backups available as well as any supplies necessary to keep these items in good working order for as long as possible.

3. Clothes and Shoes

I realize there were cobblers and seamstresses once upon a time, but these are becoming lost skills. I honestly doubt I could sew a proper shirt if I had to. Besides, it's not like the fabric that you need to make clothes comes out of thin air since it must be gathered and processed, too, and I don't have a clue how to do any of that.

Makeshift shoes are easier to piece together than clothing but cobbling together a suitable set of footwear for rugged, long-term use is something altogether different. Ensure you have a quality pair of work or hiking boots and snow boots if necessary.

Let's not forget those of us who have growing kids. Do you have enough clothing and shoes they can grow into for years to come? Remember that kids grow fast, which means they may quickly outgrow what you expect them to use. Scour at Goodwill and similar secondhand stores for deals.

Remember to include:

- Insulated gloves, thick socks, and stocking caps for winter;
- General safety gear, such as safety glasses, hearing protection, a hard hat, and plenty of rugged gloves for outdoor work;
- Any specialty personal protection equipment, like chaps for chainsaw work, a safety belt for climbing trees, or a bee suit for beekeeping.

4. Ammunition

While it's quite possible to reload ammunition, it's tedious work and you still need the supplies and equipment to do so properly and safely. If these were normal times, then I would suggest you simply purchase plenty of the ammunition you could expect to use since it will last a lifetime if kept dry. Presently, ammunition is in short supply or marked up considerably, so you're going to have to wait for prices to come down or pay a hefty premium. When they do return to normal, purchase what you think you'll need and then buy more.

5. Fuel

I see long-term reliance on equipment that uses fuel (e.g., gasoline, diesel, propane, kerosene) to be difficult because these fuels will either run out, become cost-prohibitive, or both. That's not to say you shouldn't rely on a wide assortment of equipment which runs on fuel in the short-term—I certainly do—but if you build your collapse survival plan around their existence, then you're going to be in trouble when they're gone.

For the short-term you should safely stockpile as much fuel as you can, though there are often local regulations limiting how much you're allowed to store. And while you can use this stored fuel for space heating, cooking food, heating and sterilizing water, and running equipment like chainsaws or tractors, think long and hard about how you intend to use such a precious resource. Remember to store gasoline and diesel with a fuel stabilizer—I prefer PRI-G or PRI-D—and rotate your supplies to ensure it remains viable for as long as possible.

6. Batteries

Do you know how to make a battery? I sure don't. With that in mind, stockpile plenty of the smaller alkaline batteries (e.g., AA, AAA, D-cell, 9-volt) which power crucial survival gear, such as smoke alarms, weather radios, communication equipment, and flashlights. Batteries usually last for many years without worry as long as they're kept out of extreme temperatures, so there's no harm in stockpiling quite a bit. That said, it might make more sense to have the capability to recharge batteries rather than to stockpile hundreds or thousands of alkaline batteries for a collapse scenario. We'll discuss rechargeable batteries later.

7. Hand Tools

There are many hand tools and related items which could prove useful during a collapse, including:

- Carpentry tools: claw hammer, crosscut saw, hack saw, manual hand drill, wrenches, screwdrivers, pry bar, slide clamps, sawhorses;
- Gardening tools: shovel, spade, rake, hoe, mattock, hand pruner, wheelbarrow or garden cart;
- Woodworking tools: axe, hatchet, splitting maul, file set, drill bits;

- Other tools: sledgehammer, post driver, hand auger, hand siphon pump;
- Miscellaneous items: hand-crank can opener, broom and dust pan, clothesline.

Most of these items are so useful that it would be a good idea to have backups.

8. Tarps and Plastic Sheeting

Yes, I realize you can create makeshift shelters using natural elements, but tarps are so much easier and faster to use, move, and manipulate that it's wise to include several of varying sizes. Tarps between 8'x10' and 20'x30' should suffice for most scenarios. Likewise, plastic sheeting has so many survival applications that you should include a roll or two in your supplies as well.

Tarps, for example, can be used to create makeshift shelters, temporary home repairs, and blackout shades. They can be turned into makeshift awnings or used to cover your garden during potential frosts and to protect firewood. Clean tarps can also be used to collect rainwater, which will be much cleaner than your rooftop, that's for sure.

Plastic sheeting can be used similarly to tarps, though it's usually prone to rips and punctures, so you'll need to be more careful with it. With that in mind, plastic can be used for waterproofing almost anything, for rainwater collection—including as a solar still—and even for enclosing a greenhouse, though there are specialty UV-resistant plastics made explicitly for greenhouse applications. Plastic sheets can also be useful for a makeshift quarantine room or for sheltering-in-place applications as well. If you must choose between clear and black plastic, choose clear as it has more survival applications than black plastic does.

9. Writing Supplies

There may come a time when computers and keyboards no longer function, so you'll have to go back to paper and pencil to create lists for yourself, leave instructions for others, or journal your thoughts for future generations to name a few uses. You can often find spiral-bound notebooks or pads of paper inexpensively around the time of back-to-school sales. Include plenty of #2 pencils, a pencil sharpener, and several erasers and you'll be set.

10. Fire Starting Supplies

You may already know that there are dozens of remarkable ways to start a fire, from a filled water balloon or polished underside of a soda can to steel wool and a 9-volt battery, as well as plenty more ideas. But nothing you can improvise is as easy or reliable as matches or a Bic lighter. They're inexpensive, readily available, and both will last years if kept dry.

11. Construction Materials

Anything you can think of which would be useful for construction or, more likely, repairing your home is useful to stockpile. This could include nails, screws, electrical wiring, copper pipe, PVC pipe, plywood, and assorted lumber to name several obvious examples. Now, while you may be able to scavenge some of the aforementioned larger supplies post-collapse, it may be easiest to stockpile sundries, like nails and screws, now while they're abundant and inexpensive.

We've also seen lumber, copper pipe, and electrical wiring become significantly more expensive because of shortages and theft. Additionally, plywood has uses beyond home construction, such as permanently boarding up a broken window and proactively protecting windows from damage amid storms or civil unrest.

During a prolonged time of crisis, expect many of these construction materials to be worth their weight in gold.

Where to Buy Survival Items Inexpensively

I enjoy purchasing items online as much as the next guy—often from Amazon because it's cheap, easy, and fast—but there's a wealth of preparedness items out there if you only take the time to look. You'll find everything you can imagine, from fishing gear and gardening tools to water barrels and generators. It's amazing what you can find if you're persistent and patient.

Whereas I used to search Craigslist.org to find hidden bargains, lately I've had much better success on Facebook's Marketplace. What I like about Facebook is that you're always dealing with people who already have a personal account, which means you should have a better idea of who you're about to meet when you arrive. That said, it never hurts to be safe by taking all the typical precautions, such as letting a trusted family member or friend know where you're going, who you're meeting, and when you expect to return. Better yet, take someone with you.

Another great way to find hidden gems is to search local yard sales. You'll spend more time looking for useful preparedness gear, but you'll often pay less if you're willing to put in the legwork and negotiate.

Whatever you choose, remember that many of the more useful preparedness items will be in short supply during hard times. Just as with anything else, if you haven't prepared beforehand, then you're going to regret it later.

Beyond Stockpiling Supplies

While I firmly believe in gathering more of the supplies that you know you will use down the road, the list of supplies to stockpile can get very long indeed. Consider everything you and your family may already use in your daily lives, including:

- Personal hygiene supplies, such as hand soap, shampoo and conditioner, deodorant, toothpaste and floss, mouthwash, feminine hygiene products, shaving supplies, and lotion;
- Assorted household cleaners, including dish soap, laundry soap, bathroom cleaners, floor and carpet cleaners, household sprays of all sorts, and disinfectants;
- Prescription medications, over-the-counter medications, medical and first aid supplies;
- Supplies for children and babies like diapers or pull-ups, formula or baby food, and rash cream.

Clearly, the list of specific items you use will differ depending on your needs, though I'm positive there are many supplies that you make use of which you'll regret not having if they're unavailable or too expensive to purchase. Start making that list now.

Although it's relatively easy to gather the supplies you'll need since most items from the list above will be viable for years to come, you should begin to think beyond merely stockpiling what you need. Because while you can certainly purchase years' worth of personal hygiene supplies, cleaners, and some medications, I can tell you from personal experience that this isn't necessarily the best plan.

What could go wrong, you ask? For starters, it's easy to misplace supplies. As I write this, we're in the middle of moving back to the Midwest, and I can tell you that several times I've found supplies in places that I completely forgot about. Regrettably, some of my stashed supplies may no longer be good to use simply because of neglect.

Another major problem is that years turn into decades at some point. I've been prepping long enough now that I've run into supplies which are well beyond their expiration date because I've held on to them for so long. As a result, some supplies may be completely useless because I've exposed them to extreme temperatures in a non-air-conditioned garage for years. Yes, I get lazy too.

Although stockpiling the specific supplies you will use is better than not doing anything, you might actually be better off storing the raw materials to make some of the aforementioned hygiene and cleaning supplies because the raw materials typically last longer, are less expensive, and are often as effective as their pre-made equivalents.

Examples of Homemade Options

We've been making homemade household cleaners for years because they work just as good as their store-bought counterparts and are much less expensive to make. In addition, my wife likes them because they're healthier for us and better for the environment. I don't believe we'll ever not make our own household cleaners again.

Cleaning recipes can be as simple or as complex as you like. For instance, our general-purpose household cleaner is equal parts white vinegar and water with two dozen drops of lavender essential oil to make it smell better. I'd say it doesn't get much easier to make than that. Our floor cleaner is slightly more complex because it uses equal parts white vinegar, water, and isopropyl alcohol with a half teaspoon of Dawn dish soap and two dozen drops of essential oils. The glass cleaner we make uses similar ingredients to the floor cleaner.

Of course, not everything works as well as our household cleaners do. For instance, I've tried making a wide variety of other cleaners, including dishwasher liquid and laundry soap. And although they worked, the results weren't as good as those from store-bought options. I also used to make deodorant, lotion, and shampoo for a while. Eventually, laziness set in and I went back to purchasing many store-bought options, but at least I know how to make them, and you should, too.

Luckily, there are many homemade alternatives you can make with very few ingredients, the four most important of which are white vinegar, baking soda, borax, and Epsom salts. Add in a few additional supplies, such as isopropyl alcohol, coconut oil, and cornstarch, and you can make almost any cleaner or personal hygiene product you could imagine.

Of course, you'll need to know how to make it all, so I recommend you print out your favorite recipes from online resources or purchase a book or two. Realize, too, that you can make an assortment of natural products using essential oils, herbs, flowers, and more if you prefer a truly organic approach.

Alternatives to Making Your Own Supplies

As much as I enjoy making my own health and hygiene products when I can, I realize that not everyone wants to put in the effort. Truth be told, sometimes attempting to make your own just isn't workable. For example, imagine trying to make your own toilet paper or medications; that won't end well, I promise.

I'd rather just know that alternatives exist should it ever come to that. I've already mentioned alternatives to toilet paper, but what about alternatives to daily medications? What if there's an herbal supplement you could take instead of a prescription medication? At the very least, it's much easier to stockpile months or years worth of supplements than it is a prescription. As an example from my personal experience, my wife and I have found several beneficial supplements over the years that we take, and if we hadn't found them, I can almost guarantee we would be on a prescription medication or two.

Let me be clear: Although I believe there are many viable, nonprescription alternatives which exist, I understand that this may not be the case for you. If you find that you simply must have a prescription medication, then it would be wise to do everything in your power to stockpile as much of that medication as you can. Talk to your doctor, your insurance company, and your pharmacist to come up with a solution.

If it's not possible to stockpile more of your necessary medications, then you have a problem. Specifically, what happens after your medication runs out and you find it's too expensive to purchase or, worse, completely unavailable? Nothing good, that's for sure.

So, what can you do now to prepare for such a possibility? Aside from finding an alternative, natural option like herbal supplements, what if you could reduce or even reverse a chronic problem? I'm not here to give medical advice or suggest there are remedies for everything, but I will say that my family has overcome various conditions over the years by changing our lifestyle. As an example, I was borderline hypertensive for many years until I dealt with my stress via meditation and exercise. My wife was prediabetic until she began intermittent fasting. And my youngest son had eczema as a baby and toddler until we found a natural allergy elimination therapy called N.A.E.T.

I encourage you to seek alternative options now because prescriptions may be one of the most difficult items to acquire during a collapse. Remember to always discuss such matters with your doctor or healthcare practitioner because there could be reasons you and I are completely unaware of which prevent you from seeking alternatives.

Final Thoughts on Equipment to Stockpile

I encourage you to stock up on as much of the aforementioned supplies as you can while they're still available and relatively inexpensive. The list is long, but odds are that you'll use much of what you purchase now at some point. That said, don't go overboard by purchasing decades' worth of any particular item because many things can and will go bad or merely lose their efficacy over time. Of course, most supplies you use daily will last for years without worry if stored in a cool, dry place and away from light. And if you further package your supplies in a sealed container or airtight bag, then they will undoubtedly last that much longer.

I also suggest you include the raw materials to make your own personal hygiene supplies and household cleaners. Usually all you need is white vinegar, baking soda, borax, Epsom salts, isopropyl alcohol, coconut oil, and cornstarch. While not a raw material, Dawn dish soap is great to have on hand as well. Remember to include a few essential oils like lavender as well as a book of recipes and you'll have everything you need to make your own homemade cleaners and more from scratch.

Gather Vital Reference Materials

It might shock you to hear that when times get tough, the most important survival information may no longer be accessible to you. How's that possible in the internet age with downloadable e-books and print-on-demand, you ask?

It's not so much that the information may no longer be available but that people who are more capable of paying for it may price you out of the market. For instance, when hyperinflation hits, you may find that print books on homesteading or food preservation cost a hundred times what they do now. Could you afford to pay several hundred dollars for a book about canning? I sure couldn't. Or, Heaven forbid, you may encounter greedy business owners who charge for information that was once given away freely by hiding their best articles behind a membership paywall.

No doubt, you may still find hidden gems and kindhearted people who won't do this, but I wouldn't rely on luck and charity as a survival strategy. Take the time now to gain survival knowledge that could prove useful to you down the road. While print books are best, e-books are acceptable if cost is a concern. Download e-books to a trusty e-reader or laptop computer that you can keep charged using an off-grid power source if the electrical grid goes out, is unreliable, or becomes too expensive.

Which Books to Purchase?

Many books would be great to have during a collapse. I keep many survival books myself, but I suggest you concentrate on books that teach skills you may not have now or which require very specific knowledge that is easy to forget, such as canning recipes.

Focus on books about country living, homesteading, living off-grid, canning and preserving food, and medical knowledge as the primary concerns. You may also want to include books which discuss more primitive skills, such as bushcraft, wilderness survival, and edible and medicinal plants to name a few. Really, anything that explains how to do something which benefits your survival is great to have on hand. I'll include a more thorough reference here. For now, I highly recommend the following books to start:

- *The Encyclopedia of Country Living* by Carla Emery;
- *Back to Basics* by Abigail Gehring;
- *The Survival Medicine Handbook*, 3rd edition by Dr. Joseph Alton;
- *Ball Complete Book of Home Preserving* by Judi Kingry;
- *Bushcraft 101* by Dave Canterbury.

What if You Can't Afford to Purchase Dozens of Books?

While hard copy books are best, if you cannot afford a survival library at the moment, then I recommend you look for free information online. For starters, I keep an ongoing database of survival and preparedness resources on my website. You'll find free information covering a wide range of survival topics, including food storage and cooking, medical guides, personal safety, water procurement and treatment, and plenty more. It's all free, and many of the more important references I've included are PDF files which can be easily downloaded.

If you want even more resources than what I offer, then I suggest you search online for "survival PDF files" or something similar. When you do, you'll encounter sites like SeasonedCitizenPrepper.com which have already compiled links to a wide range of PDF files that may be of use. I will caution you, however, that it's easy to become overwhelmed by such information and, as a result, never take action. I can say the same for the many resources I offer on my website. Personally, I've spent days downloading and then printing material that I thought I needed but which I ultimately never read or referenced. Years later, I tossed much of what I printed in favor of simply purchasing print books which are often better references to begin with.

Ultimately, if you're going to go the route of downloading PDF files for later reference, be sensible about what you download and especially about what you print.

Learn Basic Survival Skills

Even though I recommend purchasing preparedness books for the wealth of survival knowledge contained within, nothing beats actual knowledge gained from experience. As an example, it's one thing to own a book which details how to create a tin can rocket stove yet quite another to make and use one. What about knot-tying? I own an excellent book on the topic for reference, but I also know how to tie several of the most important knots. I can say the same for many other skills which you should know, including:

- Water filtration and purification;
- Fire starting;
- Campfire cooking;
- Basic first aid;
- Building shelter.

Anything you're willing to learn now is great, though I would focus on the list above since those skills are the ones that will tend to keep you and your family healthy, well-fed, and alive.

Entertainment for Boring Times

I encourage you not to ignore entertainment ideas for a collapse scenario because the internet and all that it offers may not be available at some point. Could you imagine YouTube, Netflix, or TikTok not being around to entertain us at the press of a button? Personally, I've never watched a TikTok video, but my nearly grown children seem to watch it nonstop. Sadly, many people do the same thing these days, especially our youth.

Some of us—me included—believe it will be a good thing if we're no longer constantly inundated with such drivel, but the human brain enjoys being stimulated, so hours of boredom could negatively affect some people in the beginning of a prolonged collapse. Having something enjoyable to look forward to will be a welcome reprieve for all in the family, especially when everyone's days are now filled with seemingly monotonous chores like preparing food from scratch, hauling water, and chopping firewood.

What Entertainment Options Should You Purchase?

All the standard family leisure ideas apply:

- Board games, appropriate for age groups. Classic board games such as Monopoly, Clue, Sorry, and Scrabble come to mind. If you have young children, then games like Candy Land, Chutes and Ladders, and Operation may be better options. I'm sure there are newer games to consider as well, but these are often family favorites and hard to go wrong with.
- A multi-game set that includes chess, checkers, backgammon, and more is a superb choice and one I highly recommend.
- A simple deck of cards can entertain for hours. There are classic card games such as poker, war, solitaire, and hearts, as well as plenty of other games I've never even heard of if you want more options. Even if you know all the rules, I suggest you take the time now to print them out or, better yet, purchase a book of family card games for reference.
- Fiction books could be useful to include as well. Sometimes it's nice to read a story, even if you've already read the book previously. What to include is up to you, but

I propose a wide variety of books that would appeal to people besides yourself. Often yard sales are a great place to purchase books for pennies on the dollar, but if you're looking for something specific, then search online.

What About Videos?

It may also prove beneficial to purchase videos of your favorite movies and television shows, particularly if you have young children who have their current favorite shows that they cannot live without. Young children can watch the same thing repeatedly, which, although grueling for parents, may be beneficial when you need to focus on something else for a while. And while I'm not a huge fan of using the television as a babysitter, if I'm being honest, it was nice when I could sit my children down to watch a movie while I did something else for an hour.

Now, while it may tempt you to download dozens of Netflix movies to your tablet or smartphone, realize that these movies expire relatively quickly; the same is true for YouTube video downloads even if you have a premium subscription, as well as for Amazon Prime videos. I believe nearly all video downloads expire within thirty days no matter the provider you use, so they aren't a viable option.

Perhaps the only sustainable alternative is to purchase DVDs. Luckily, you can often find classic children's movies for cheap in store discount bins and yard sales. Personally, I wouldn't go overboard purchasing movies that may never get watched since children grow up and change interests quickly. There's also no guarantee that you'll even be able to play DVD movies if electricity prices skyrocket or the power grid becomes unreliable. It's merely mentioned here because many children can't live without their daily fix of cartoons or Disney movies.

Final Thoughts on Reference Materials

Like I said at the start of this chapter, don't assume such vital knowledge will always be available to you. Yes, we've become accustomed to unlimited and immediate answers at our fingertips, but that might not always be the case. Take the time now to gather the books and information you'll need to survive hard times, especially books that teach skills or which contain difficult-to-remember information, like canning recipes. I recommend you focus on country living, homesteading, living off-grid, canning and preserving food, and medical knowledge as the primary areas of interest.

In addition, developing lifelong survival skills is always a great idea no matter how many books you purchase. Focus on water purification, fire starting, campfire cooking, basic first aid, and shelter building because the more you know, the less you need.

Don't ignore entertainment options either. Get a few board games, a deck of cards, and an all-in-one game kit and you'll have hundreds of hours of quality family entertainment. Remember that entertainment isn't solely for your family or young children but for you as well. Yes, you may very well be busier than usual, but you'll still appreciate the occasional break. And if you can do something fun when times get tough, then all the better.

7 Primary Survival Concerns

Aside from the crucial topics we've already covered, there are seven major areas of collapse survival that you should pay special attention to, including addressing health concerns, proper sanitation and hygiene, the ability to cook, keep warm, light up the darkness, alternative power, and security.

Physical Fitness and Health Problems

If you're physically out of shape or have health concerns that you've been putting off, now's the time to address these issues if possible. Clearly, there are chronic health problems that can only be managed, but, as I mentioned previously, there are some concerns which can be eased or reduced with significant changes to your lifestyle. Yes, it's not always easy, but I promise your body will thank you now as well as when hard times come.

At minimum, take the time now to fix common ailments that most of us have, such as dental work you may have been putting off, eyesight concerns which may be fixed with procedures like LASIK, or joint trouble that requires surgery to name a few. Whatever you can take care of now, before these medical options are no longer available or too costly, is good to get done.

As with any medical advice, discuss all major plans with your doctor, even a new fitness regimen, because you could have underlying health concerns that may prevent you from doing something you thought was good for you. Or, it's equally possible that a modification to your plans is a better solution for your situation; your doctor would know best.

Sanitation and Hygiene

Diseases caused by a lack of sanitation have been among the top killers of humans throughout history. Some of the worst diseases include cholera, diarrhea, dysentery, hepatitis A, typhoid, and polio. The bottom line is that you need to keep yourself clean from head to toe and your waste products need to be properly disposed of immediately.

Regarding proper hygiene, it starts with clean water and judicious use of soap. Beyond that, you need to bathe yourself regularly, which may be challenging if you're also trying to conserve water for consumption. Assuming you have enough water to clean yourself each day, use a sponge or washcloth to clean areas that get dirty quickly, particularly your face, hands, feet, armpits, and groin.

Your feet and armpits, in particular, deserve special attention because they sweat more, which causes the skin to get irritated quicker and, therefore, result in trouble which could sideline you for days or weeks on end. Try to wash yourself at night so you remove all the accumulated bacteria and other nasties that cause problems before bed unless you became exceptionally dirty during the day.

Cooking Food

As I've mentioned several times already, the power grid may be unreliable so you may not be able to use the stovetop or oven to cook with. In that case, you'll need to seek alternatives, such as a wood-burning stovetop during the winter, an outdoor campfire during the summer, or a number of solar cooker designs for when the sun is out.

Not only have I built a makeshift solar cooker from scraps that, with a few tweaks, would reliably work to boil water, but I've used an All-American Sun Oven for years to cook everything from fish and pizza to soups and stews and even a cobbler. I can't think of a better free way to cook food if you live somewhere that gets adequate sunlight much of the year. The Pacific Northwest, where I currently live, isn't the best location for solar oven cooking, though there are still plenty of sunny days that make building one a sensible choice.

While I recognize that most people will instinctively resort to their backyard grill, you need to appreciate that both propane and charcoal may be difficult to acquire as time goes on. Firewood, on the other hand, is renewable and, more importantly, acquirable by you with little more than a saw or axe. Of course, you won't be felling trees, and I wouldn't recommend it unless you know what you're doing, but you should still be able to gather what you need for basic cooking purposes if you live anywhere there's an abundance of trees.

What About Heating Water?

Although you may be tempted to build a campfire to heat water for bathing or cooking purposes, don't do that unless you have no other choice. Instead, use a solar camp shower or build a passive solar shower, then place it out in the sun for a few hours and you'll get hot water most days during the summer months, warm water during the spring and fall, and probably not freezing cold water in the winter. Hey, not everything works like a charm.

Heating water during the winter can get tricky and time-consuming. If you have a wood-burning stove, use that to heat pots of water. Solar water heating ideas can help to preheat water, but they usually won't get water hot in the winter. You can purchase a boiler for heating both your home and water, but that's expensive and typically only for completely off-grid situations. Some people use solar systems and on-demand tanks for heating water, but they're expensive as well. And I wouldn't recommend using propane or charcoal for this purpose either.

Ultimately, we're down to building an outdoor campfire for most of us. The good news is that you don't have to get a roaring fire going. Even a small rocket stove with twigs will boil a cup of water. Or build any number of other makeshift stove designs and boil or cook almost anything. If you prefer to purchase a rocket stove, the Solo Stove or EcoZoom Versa Camping Stove are always great choices.

But if you want something different or larger, just search "rocket stove" on Amazon and you'll find plenty of options. I suggest you stick with smaller designs as they are typically more efficient for most cooking purposes, can use smaller pieces of wood, which makes gathering firewood easier on you, and are less expensive.

Keeping Warm

Most of us are completely unaccustomed to being truly cold in the winter. We prefer a balmy seventy-two degrees and readily complain if somebody nudges the thermostat. On a personal note, my teenage children still believe they should be able to run around in shorts all winter long; they, along with so many others, will have a rude awakening coming.

So, what should you do? Start with clothing for cold weather indoor use. This should include an insulated coat or jacket, insulated gloves that aren't overly bulky so that you don't lose dexterity, wool or insulated socks, a quality stocking cap, and even long underwear as a base layer if it gets cold enough where you live. Remember that we're not trying to prepare for being outdoors for hours on end with this clothing, though you should certainly have clothing that can be used outdoors. Rather, this clothing is something you can expect to rely upon day in and day out for indoor use, so it should be relatively comfortable and flexible yet durable.

For bedtime, have plenty of blankets or comforters. Sleeping bags are great to include as well; often you can find them in great condition at yard sales for cheap. Another idea is to bundle up with other people to share body heat. You can even heat a water bottle on a wood stove during the evening and bring it to bed with you, placing the bottle by your feet to keep warm.

While there are plenty of alternative heating options, such as passive solar heaters, wood boilers, rocket mass heaters, and pellet stoves, these options are impractical for most homeowners or expensive. My advice is to stick with a wood stove as the easiest option. Now, while a pellet stove may be more efficient, wood is more easily renewable on your own, which is a crucial consideration with any heating option you choose. If you don't already have a wood stove, then it either doesn't get cold enough where you live or you should invest in one if you have no intention of moving soon.

Assuming you have a wood stove or some form of supplemental heat, then you're going to be living in that room for some time. Pull up a sleeping bag and mattress and get comfortable. You should conserve heat loss by erecting insulating barriers over large windows and closing off heat escape into other rooms by hanging a comforter or even a tarp over large openings. Remember that airflow is still necessary, so don't go overboard by trying to seal up every crack and crevice.

Last, please don't do anything unsafe to heat your home or cook with indoors. Some heating ideas can be dangerous to you, and the last thing you want is to find your home has burned down because you did something ill-advised. Similarly, never use any outdoor stove indoors, particularly charcoal grills, because they all give off carbon monoxide due to the incomplete combustion of their fuel source. Using such stoves indoors can and will kill you. I can say the same for running a generator indoors, even in a partially enclosed garage, because of the deadly fumes. Keep outdoor stoves and items outside where they belong, even in the winter.

Lighting Ideas

We've become entirely reliant on artificial light in our modern society, but there's a simple strategy to reduce your lighting needs during a collapse: Go to bed when it gets dark and get up when the sun rises. Yes, it's a novel idea, but one that humanity has employed for much of our existence. And, throughout most of the year, it works wonders.

If you still insist on having light sources for when it gets dark—and who doesn't—I suggest battery-powered LED flashlights and lanterns. While there are certainly brighter lantern options available which rely on propane and kerosene, these are fuels that, as I've mentioned previously, will run out relatively quickly. And while I fully recognize disposable batteries will run out as well, the efficiency of battery-powered lights these days is phenomenal. Plus, most alkaline batteries will last for a decade or more without worry. But if that's not enough, then purchase plenty of Eneloop rechargeable batteries and have the capability to recharge them and you'll have a nearly indefinite power source for all your lighting needs for years to come.

Last, consider purchasing a solar-powered lantern that can be recharged each day when not needed as well as a hand-crank light called the NowLight, which generates hours worth of light with a single minute of pulling the cord. Unlike traditional hand-crank lights and radios, the NowLight is truly an efficient use of human energy.

Alternative Power

Should you invest in wind, hydro, solar, geothermal, or some combination of them? As with anything related to collapse survival, diversification is preferable, though it's difficult for the average prepper to opt for anything besides solar or wind.

The question, really, is whether you should opt for a whole-house solar system or something smaller? I'd say a whole-house system is the way to go if all the following apply:

1. You can afford the upfront cost of, on average, $50,000 for an off-grid system. That's a ballpark estimate since your costs will vary considerably depending on a variety of factors like the manufacturer you go with and whether you do the work yourself or contract it out. To make solar power more affordable, many companies offer monthly

payment plans and then there are government incentives to consider. But let's not forget that there are scammers everywhere, even in the solar industry; read the fine print and scour customer reviews before committing to anything.
2. You have no intention of moving and you already live somewhere relatively away from major population centers, even the suburbs. If not, I'm afraid a whole-house solar power system will only become a beacon for the unprepared masses.
3. You feel you simply must continue to run every appliance, television, and light in the house. Realize that water may be scarce, internet and cable television may be too costly, and it is possible to ration power consumption from one use to the next, thereby significantly reducing your needs.

If the above doesn't fit your situation, then a simple small-scale solar system may be the best option because you'll still be able to power most of your crucial equipment such as a large refrigerator, small electronics, and even power tools with relatively little initial cost. The biggest problem is learning to be judicious with your power usage since you usually won't be able to power more than one item at a time.

Consider Small-Scale Wind Power

I'm a fan of solar power, but I realize solar isn't workable for every situation. For example, it rains or is cloudy much of the winter in the Pacific Northwest. Here, small-scale wind power setup may prove far more useful than solar. If wind power interests you then [this video playlist](#) by Missouri Wind and Solar is a good start.

Understand, too, that it is possible to combine wind and solar. In fact, using both wind and solar may be the best solution because you'll have built-in redundancy and maximize resource usage.

Get Your Power Usage Down

Reducing your daily power needs is always the best first step no matter whether you can afford a whole-house system or not. As an example, an energy star refrigerator can reduce electricity consumption to a fraction of a 1980s-era refrigerator. But if you only need to power a mini fridge for your meats and dairy, you'll often use less than half of the power an energy start refrigerator consumes. You can further reduce consumption by using LED light bulbs, powering a laptop or tablet instead of a desktop computer, and eliminating vampire loads—electronics that continue to use power even when not turned on—as a few ideas. Reduce consumption even further by passively heating water, using alternative methods to heat your home, and cooking with renewables like firewood.

Security and Defense

A proper discussion of all that's possible regarding your home security and personal defense is a lot to tackle here. That said, you cannot ignore such a crucial area of your preparedness plan, and you shouldn't do it alone, which is why I believe in finding like-minded people who see the world as you do, especially if they're family, friends, and neighbors. In any case, there's a lot you can do to harden your home and prepare for a time without rule of law. Aside from firearms ownership and watching videos on home defense and security, my two biggest book recommendations include: *Prepper's Home Defense* by Jim Cobb and *Contact!* by Max Velocity.

Final Thoughts on 7 Primary Survival Concerns

If you get these seven concerns squared away before collapse occurs and you've got a good plan for procuring food and water, odds are that you'll have a good chance of not only surviving whatever comes but thriving while others falter. Because, let's face it, most people don't have a clue how to stay warm or keep the lights on when the grid goes down, let alone how to keep themselves safe when everyone else loses their minds.

And they tend not to deal with problems until they're forced to, so you'll be ahead of the curve because you dealt with your health concerns and you'll have a plan in place for keeping clean and healthy while everyone else gets sick.

Add in some form of a alternative power system, even if it's a small system, and you'll have your basic power needs covered. Finally, so long as you can continue to cook food and heat water—both for your safety and for your comfort—life should continue relatively uninterrupted, if not be a lot busier.

9 Additional Considerations

Please don't gloss over my final recommendations because we're only now addressing them. These considerations are more important than most people realize, especially if they apply to your situation.

Children and Pets

Those most reliant on you for their survival—children and pets—need little more than the same things you do for their survival, particularly food, water, and shelter. Young children will need some additional items to make things easier, such as:

- **Diapers or pull-ups**. At some point disposable diapers will run out, so you should invest in reusable diapers or learn how to make your own.
- **Formula and baby food**, or know how to make your own baby food.
- **Medications** appropriate for their age. You don't want to dose children with adult medications.
- **Educational supplies**. Books, writing supplies, pencils, and more are good to include.
- **Toys**. Yes, they still need entertainment and stimulation.

Pets, too, certainly need food. While most dry food will stay good for many months, even years, I would still suggest storing it just like any other bulk food you might store for yourself. At some point, though, you'll need to learn to make your own pet food at home.

Pest Control is Vital to Your Health

Ants, cockroaches, fleas, ticks, flies, mosquitoes, mice, rats, and racoons may all become a serious problem during a collapse scenario. Think about how much trouble we have controlling these pests when there's running water, flushing toilets, garbage removal, an array of household cleaners and insecticides, and commercial pest control services. Now consider how bad they'll be when none of the above control measures exist and your neighbors are doing everything wrong. It will become a mess, that's for sure.

Realize, too, that many of the aforementioned pests carry diseases:

- Ticks carry several diseases, including Lyme disease and Rocky Mountain spotted fever.
- Mosquitoes transmit West Nile virus, heartworm (a big problem for dogs), and malaria (this is usually only a problem outside the United States).
- Fleas carry typhus, tapeworms, and more.
- Cockroaches spread diseases such as dysentery and cholera as well as intestinal parasites.
- Racoons could be rabid, and their feces are home to an assortment of bacteria and viruses like E. coli and salmonella.
- Rodents carry hantavirus, leptospirosis, and rat-bite fever.
- Bird droppings carry many diseases, including salmonella, leptospirosis, and encephalitis.
- Ticks, fleas, and rats can all carry the plague.

The list of harmful diseases is much longer than what I've included here, though I hope you understand just how important it is to keep pests and insects under control.

While you can and should stockpile plenty of insecticides, rodent traps, and fly traps, the most important action you can take is to reduce the likelihood of your home and surroundings becoming a breeding ground. This means you must keep your home clean inside and out, dispose of trash by burying or burning it, and quickly deal with problems when they arise rather than allow them to fester.

Why Bartering is a Bad Idea

I'm not a big fan of bartering during a collapse for two main reasons. First, preparing to barter may encourage you to purchase items you'll never use instead of supplies you know you'll need at some point. For example, you may choose to purchase high-demand items like alcohol, cigarettes, and coffee beans because you know people will pay top dollar for them during a collapse when you could've spent that money on more toilet paper, medicines, and soap—all supplies you'll surely use down the road.

Second, I believe attempting to barter, at least early on, places your safety at risk because you put yourself out there as somebody who has excess supplies and, therefore, likely has much more stashed away at home. It wouldn't take long for the wrong people to follow you home only to overwhelm you and demand everything you have. Of course, it is possible to barter through a trusted third party, such as a priest, but that has disadvantages as well.

As the collapse continues and the population sorts itself out, I expect the most civilized and prepared people to remain standing. Eventually, bartering will become a viable means of exchange, but not initially. Last, I would never suggest purchasing supplies you'll never use for this purpose; it's just a waste of money, time, and storage space.

Building Relationships is Essential

When I first began prepping many years ago, I was against the idea of preparing with other people, mainly because I kept hearing from friends and family that they would "come to my house" when times got tough. To me that meant they had no interest in preparing themselves and, instead, expected me to care for them because they would rather spend their money on new cars and yearly vacations. It would be like me saying to them, "I chose not to save for retirement, so share your 401(k) with me."

Over the years, I've convinced a few close friends and family members to prepare themselves, but not many. I'm afraid you either understand the need to prepare or you don't, which brings me to your dilemma: Do you choose to go it alone and attempt survival on your own, or do you suck it up and invite others into your home, knowing full well that they bring little supplies and skills with them?

Like I said, I was very much against the idea of taking in the unprepared, but as I've gotten older, I've softened my attitude for three main reasons:

1. As I age, I find myself less able to perform physical labor for hours on end. And, as you might suspect, there will be plenty of manual tasks that need done during a collapse.
2. I'm only one person. I can't chop firewood to heat the house, maintain a fire for hours on end to cook food and boil water, and spend hours making food from scratch all by myself. Yes, my wife can help but our days will be busier than I prefer if it's just us. Having other adults around who can help with these chores and others like them will be welcome.
3. There's safety in numbers. As much as I want to believe we'll go undetected and stay safe, there's no guarantee. In fact, it's highly likely that we will be targeted at some point. Personally, I would rather have other men around who can help me fend off attackers than attempt to do so myself.

Remember that you're wanting to foster relationships with people you can trust and who you know will be useful when times are tough. This isn't about taking in whoever shows up at your doorstep, as I'm sure there are friends and family you'd be less than enthused to take in. Regardless, you'll have to make the hard decision to allow these people in or not.

Understand that whomever you open your doors to, you'll want to set firm expectations and hard boundaries so there's no confusion as to what's expected of them and, more importantly, so you have cause to remove those who are no longer helpful.

Last, building relationships isn't only about your friends and family. Look to your neighbors and even beyond for like-minded people. Odds are that some of them see the world as you do and will happily band together to survive the collapse. Just ensure they bring plenty to the table as well, specifically their own supplies, skills, knowledge, and work ethic.

Learn to Do With Less or Without

We as Americans have had it easy over the past century. Even despite the occasional setback like the Great Depression or a world war, most of us have had things far too easy to be mentally prepared for what's coming, particularly given all of the conveniences contemporary society affords us. Considering that most of us rarely worry about where to get food for our family, whether our water is clean, or if we're going to survive a cold night, that should be enough to prove just how easy we have things. But if you add in the fact that we have ready access to an array of life-saving medications, especially antibiotics, as well as almost anything we could imagine on the internet, I'd say we've forgotten what it's like to do without.

And as much as you and I have been working to avoid it, we may have to learn how to do with less or without despite our best efforts to the contrary. Understand that this could include almost anything you're accustomed to having an abundance of, such as food, medications, clothing, fuel, and more.

Therefore, I want you to consider a change in mindset. At a minimum, ponder what it might be like if you could not get something you need and what you might do if you couldn't. I'll remind you that we had a small glimpse of what it might be like during the great toilet paper shortage of 2020. With that in mind, if you cannot replenish your supplies at some point, ask yourself:

Will You Ration What's Remaining?

Some supplies may be easier to ration than others. For example, you may find less need for seasonings and toothpaste than medications, but just how far will you take your rationing efforts? As an example, will you use half as much toothpaste or only brush your teeth once a day? What happens when you get dangerously low on toothpaste? Will you forego using toothpaste at all?

If something is vital to your survival—like prescription medications—do your best to stockpile as much as you can now, and then consider alternatives if you must. If that's not possible, will you take half as much of your medication, skip a dose, or what? These are important considerations to contemplate now.

Is There an Effective Alternative?

If things are bad for long enough, then we're all going to be looking for viable alternatives to the supplies we've grown accustomed to using. Toilet paper is the quintessential example. Most people will figure something out, but it never hurts to have a list of alternatives where possible. I can say the same for any of the many supplies we've discussed already, including alternative cleaners, personal hygiene supplies, and medications.

How Important is What You're Missing?

Not everything is equally important to your survival. I'd suggest prescription medications are significantly more crucial than writing supplies. But where do vitamins and batteries fall on the hierarchy of needs for you? You'll have to decide that, though I would encourage you to develop a list of the more crucial items you feel you can't live without and then stockpile as much of these crucial items as you can.

Do You Truly Need More or Merely Believe You Do?

This is where your mindset truly changes. As I said earlier, we've become so accustomed to having an abundance of supplies that we've forgotten what it's like to do without. Here are a few thoughts:

- Some studies suggest you don't need toothpaste to brush your teeth, and there are ways to clean your teeth without a toothbrush if you must, though I suggest being able to brush your teeth like normal.
- You can live with a minor headache as well as most irritations that over-the-counter medications alleviate.
- Deodorant isn't necessary, though usually appreciated by others.

Whether you truly need more is a crucial question to ask before things get bad because once they do, your options become limited very quickly; you'll go straight from rationing to creative alternatives in no time flat. For most of us, that's nothing to look forward to. As much as I hate to be the bearer of bad news, the time of abundance will be over when we collapse. Now may be the time to learn to do with less before you're forced to.

Unnecessary Supplies and Actions

There are a few things you don't need to have or do for collapse survival, and you might be surprised by some of my thoughts. But I'll start with the most obvious one: You don't need to leave the United States to survive our collapse. While Americans will have a more troublesome time during an economic collapse, most other countries will be affected to one degree or another by a meltdown of the world's reserve currency. And, like it or not, most other civilized countries have their own fiat money problems which will surely rear up when we collapse. The world is living on borrowed money, and nobody will be immune.

Second, you may have noticed that underground bunker sales are at all-time highs. Contrary to dramatized television shows, bunkers aren't going to save you when things get bad. Yes, you may be able to hide for a while, but people will eventually find you. In my opinion, it's better to stay above ground and prepare to survive with people you can trust. Besides, you can only comfortably and safely house so many people in a bunker given constrained water and air filtration capabilities, and that's to say nothing of having limited space for food and supplies. Plus, at some point, you're going to go stir-crazy being stuck in a bunker for weeks or months on end.

Third, you don't necessarily need a bug out bag, at least not initially, and that's coming from somebody who's written a book on the topic. Why? Because there's going to be nowhere to run to when we collapse. Unless you have a bug out retreat you can walk to, you're going to want to stay put and survive where you are. Granted, there are scenarios in which you may need to retreat from your home, such as during a wildfire scare, so you should have some plan in place to escape should it come to that. Just focus on everything else first and worry about a bug out bag or bug out retreat when the time comes.

Living in an Apartment or Condominium

Surviving the coming collapse will be hard enough, but compounding the problem by also living in proximity to others will make things even more problematic for the simple fact that most of these people will be completely unprepared. Now, while I've also written a book on the topic of small space preparedness for natural disasters, I'm afraid collapse survival is in an entirely different ballpark regarding time frames of returning to normal which means that everyone, including your closest neighbors, may react even more irrationally.

But the problem of living in an apartment or condominium during a collapse is even more troublesome than having too many irrational nearby neighbors because you'll likely have a smaller amount land for gardening or raising livestock, less indoor space for stockpiling supplies, and fewer natural resources, like trees and rivers, to rely upon. That said, if a majority of your neighbors choose to leave at some point—and let's hope they do—then you could end up with quite a bit of space to utilize, but I wouldn't bet on being so lucky as a survival strategy.

Ultimately, I'd say that attempting to survive our collapse in an apartment or condominium is ill-advised. But, if you truly have nowhere else you can go, then building relationships is crucial. Find out who else sees the world like you do, calmly attempt to convert those who don't, and then do your best to put plans in place now that give you the greatest chance of survival.

If You Cannot Financially Afford to Prepare

Let's say you're unable to buy gold and silver or Bitcoin, you can't afford to homestead or raise livestock, and stockpiling years worth of bulk food and other supplies is out of reach because you simply don't have the funds to make it happen. What now? All is not lost, I promise. But you can't sit back and do nothing. Although people have figured out how to survive with very little in the way of resources for all of human history, there are just some things that you cannot do without, particularly food and water.

As mentioned previously, search local garage sales and online via Facebook and Craigslist. If you're patient yet willing to act quickly when the opportunity arises, you can often find people giving away useful survival items like water barrels and food, simply because they're moving. For instance, I searched Facebook's Marketplace today for the term "bulk food" and found people giving away or inexpensively selling buckets of sealed dry bulk foods, cases of camping food, dog food, and more. I then searched for the term "water barrel" and found people selling 55-gallon drums for cheap; sometimes I've even found people giving them away.

Granted, what you uncover may be less than ideal, need plenty of cleaning, or you may have to drive some distance, but if you can find great deals with a little effort, then I would strongly encourage you to take advantage of them. I can say the same for almost any survival items that one can imagine. Take your time searching, ask friends and family if they have anything you can make use of, and even consider placing want ads on Craigslist or the local paper; you might be surprised at what you come up with.

Of course, your survival isn't only about food and water or amassing a myriad of supplies. It's very much about your skills and knowledge post-collapse. If you can make yourself valuable because of what you know or what you can do then you'll have an easier time of finding work and, therefore, being able to afford the goods and services you've come to expect. The best part is that gaining knowledge now often doesn't cost a penny.

Bringing Everything Together

Perhaps you feel like you've been hit upside the head with a sledgehammer. Not only is it sinking in that an economic collapse is imminent, but now you have what feels like a thousand things to do before then. I get it; I'm in the same boat now that we're moving back home to the Midwest during a less-than-opportune time. But all is not lost. You and I can make it happen, and I'm willing to bet there's still time so long as we focus. With that in mind, where should you begin?

Start with diversifying your assets. If you've never invested in precious metals or cryptocurrencies, now's a great time to give them a shot. But I wouldn't suggest dumping all your U.S. dollars at once. Take some time to do this wisely while you also purchase an assortment of real hard assets with your fiat dollars, specifically gardening items, firearms, cookstoves, solar equipment, lamps and lanterns, construction tools, and homesteading equipment.

Remember not to store all your alternative currencies in one place. Use the bank for some of it, a safe deposit box for a bit more, and a sturdy fireproof safe hidden away in your home for the rest. In order to ensure you're as prepared as possible, develop useful skills that people will want post-collapse. If you have none, now's the time to learn something that interests you.

Now, if you live anywhere near a large city or a suburb, you should consider moving away, much further away. But as you well know, the middle of 2021 is a horrible time to purchase a home since the housing market is out of control. But if you can afford to do so, getting away from any major population center is a wise move. Even if it means you only purchase a small plot of land and build an off-grid cabin as a bug out retreat, well, that's better than staying put.

Understand, however, that history has shown the average person will walk several miles off the beaten path—specifically interstates and major highways—in their desperation to find food and supplies. Therefore, you'll want to look for a bug out location that is as far away from major thoroughfares as is feasible. Luckily, land is significantly less expensive to purchase further away from civilization, though it may be difficult to find something suitable for homestead use.

If you cannot afford to move right now, which I completely understand, then building a community of like-minded people—maybe even friends and family—who you can attempt to survive with is the next best option. And even if you can move now, it's a good idea to find people you want to survive with because the more connections you forge now, the better off you'll be when times get tough.

Once you've found family, friends, and neighbors to rely upon, you need to determine who brings what to the table. Remember that it's not only about involving people who bring more equipment and supplies with them; often you'll want to include people who have specific skills or knowledge—like medical knowledge or trade skills—as well as those who are willing to work hard in exchange for shelter and food. In essence, you're trying to build a community of people you can trust when it comes down to your survival.

Food procurement and preservation is usually the next major concern because there's so much to consider. As with preparing financially, diversification is the key. Yes, stockpiling food to see you through the initial lean times is wise, but that will only take you so far. You really need to come up with ways to procure more food year after year. Whether that means a vegetable garden, hunting, trapping, foraging, raising animals, or some combination of these, I suggest you figure out your plan now because it will all become more difficult during hard times.

Although we discussed food first, water is absolutely crucial to your survival. If you're not homesteading or unable to drill a well, rainwater harvesting is the next best option for most of us. Do everything you can to collect as much rainwater as possible and then conserve what you collect. Understand how to clean dishes, wash yourself, and wash laundry with very little water. Remember that all collected water should be considered unfit for human consumption, so you should have the capability of purifying everything you collect.

Moving on to supplies, there's so much you could stockpile that I won't attempt to rehash it all here. Suffice it to say, if you use something on a regular basis—particularly personal hygiene supplies, medications, and cleaners—then I would encourage you to buy as much as you feasibly can and then have the ability to make more from scratch using basic recipes. While you're at it, do your best to stock up on everything else you could make use of, from clothing and batteries to toilet paper and pest control.

Understand, too, that your survival isn't only about equipment and supplies; it's very much about what you know, whether that's knowledge you already possess or that which you can find in books and other reference materials. Add plenty of useful books to your library on country living, homesteading, living off-grid, canning and preserving food, and medical knowledge while they're still readily available and relatively inexpensive. You should also include a variety of entertainment options, like board games and card games, and you'll have nearly everything covered that you or your family could want or need regarding leisure activities.

Deal with your physical fitness and health concerns now, at least as much as possible. You're also going to need one or more ways to cook food, heat water, keep warm, produce light, power essential equipment, and keep your family safe. Review the seven primary survival concerns as a refresher.

Sanitation, personal hygiene, and pest control are all crucial concerns not to be ignored. Failure to adequately prepare for them is far more likely to kill you—assuming you live far enough away—than the unprepared masses. Have plenty of supplies to deal with these concerns as well as plans in place to keep yourself and your home clean and sanitary.

Finally, let's not forget about our children because they are the primary reason most of us preppers do what we do. Without a future for our children to inherit, it's difficult to imagine any of this being worth doing. I, for one, firmly believe that preparing for collapse—whatever it looks like—is well worth doing for the sake of our children, the sake of our nation, and even for the sake of humanity.

Get Your Free Checklist Here

Before you grab your checklist, be a good friend or family member and choose to help others who could use this crucial information.

Spread the Word, Share the Knowledge

I'm willing to bet that you have family and friends who could benefit from this book as well, so please take a moment right now and quickly share a link to it on Facebook, Twitter, or Pinterest. You can easily do so here.

Now, download your free, easy-to-reference, 47-point collapse checklist here. Or, if you prefer, the entire checklist is reproduced here for your convenience.

Understand What Collapse Looks Like

1. Know the signs of economic collapse: growing government debt, rising consumer debt, interest rate uncertainty, a slowing global economy, and political turmoil.
2. Know what happens during a collapse: widespread unemployment and resulting poverty and hunger, high bankruptcy rates, massive crime waves, hyperinflation, and social chaos.
3. Remember lessons from the Great Depression: eating habits change, make do with what you have, use cheaper supplies to stretch your food budget, be creative with how you use what you have (e.g., lining shoes with cardboard), use it all to the last drop (e.g., bits of soap)and save everything for later use (e.g., scraps of clothing, buttons, string), everyone pitches in, and neighbors help each other.

Prepare Yourself Financially

1. Reduce unnecessary debt and frivolous purchases. Use that money to purchase preparedness items and supplies that you typically wouldn't buy (e.g., large water containers, gardening tools, solar power equipment, firearms, etc.).
2. Invest in gold and silver coins, especially smaller denominations for barter.
3. Consider foreign currencies as an alternative to U.S. dollars, particularly the euro, the Australian dollar, the Swiss francs, and the Chinese yuan.
4. Invest in cryptocurrencies, especially Bitcoin and maybe Ethereum or possibly Litecoin.
5. Continue to hold some U.S. dollars in cash, but reduce money in your bank account. Consider stashing your alternative assets (precious metals and foreign dollars) in a safe deposit box and a sturdy home fireproof safe.
6. Develop useful skills for barter, including any medical profession, skilled trade, auto mechanic, or construction. If you don't have those skills, consider what else you can do or know, such as sewing, hunting, trapping, gunsmithing, and so on.
7. Invest in real hard assets: construction tools, hand tools, anything used around a homestead, outdoor stoves, a quality grain grinder, and so on.

Food Acquisition and Preservation

1. Stockpile store-bought food for lean times, including nutritious shelf-stable foods that provide most of your vitamin and mineral needs, bulk foods that act as filler and provide calories, and "superfoods" to supplement your nutritional intake (see book for specifics).

2. Grow food for hard times by planting a vegetable garden, fruit trees, and fruit bushes. Then learn to save seeds.
3. Raise food for independence, such as chickens, ducks, and rabbits. Move on to larger animals when you're ready, like goats, cows, and hogs. Consider adding tilapia via aquaponics.
4. If you hunt, trap, or forage, great! If you don't, get to know somebody who does.
5. Be able to preserve your harvest via home canning, dehydrating, or freeze-drying.
6. Build a root cellar or other cold storage solution.
7. Store bulk foods for the long-term using food grade buckets or Mylar bags with oxygen absorbers.

Water is Crucial to Survival

1. Drill a water well if possible.
2. Invest in large rainwater harvesting containers, such as IBC totes or cisterns.
3. Invest in a quality gravity water filter with plenty of extra filters.
4. Ration water primarily for human consumption and personal hygiene, planning on five gallons of water per person per day as the bare minimum to stockpile.
5. Reduce water usage by learning to take a Navy shower, washing dishes with the three-pot method, and doing laundry by hand.
6. Remember water for pets, farm animals, and a vegetable garden.

Equipment and Supplies to Stockpile

1. Stockpile all the supplies you might use, such as hand soap, shampoo and conditioner, deodorant, toothpaste

and floss, mouthwash, feminine hygiene products, shaving supplies, lotion, dish soap, laundry soap, bathroom cleaners, floor and carpet cleaners, household sprays of all sorts, disinfectants, prescription medications, over-the-counter medications, medical and first aid supplies, as well as supplies for children and babies like diapers or pull-ups, formula or baby food, and rash cream.
2. Continue with the essentials that are hard to make post-collapse: OTC medications, glasses, contacts, hearing aids, clothes and shoes, ammunition, fuel, batteries, hand tools, tarps and plastic sheeting, writing supplies, fire starting supplies, and construction materials.
3. Make use of online marketplaces like Facebook Marketplace to find survival items inexpensively.
4. Be able to make your own homemade household cleaners and personal hygiene items using white vinegar, baking soda, borax, Epsom salts, and isopropyl alcohol; print off recipes or purchase a book.
5. Consider alternative options, such as alternatives to toilet paper and medications.

Gather Vital Reference Materials

1. Purchase books about country living, homesteading, living off-grid, canning and preserving food, and medical knowledge as the primary concerns.
2. If you cannot afford a library of books, find resources online to download and print.
3. Learn basic survival skills, including water filtration and purification, fire starting, campfire cooking, basic first aid, and building shelters.
4. Remember entertainment for boring times, such as board games, a multi-game set, a deck of cards, and fiction books. Ignore videos unless you simply must have them.

7 Primary Concerns for Collapse Survival

1. Deal with your health problems; get physically fit.
2. Proper sanitation and hygiene is a must. Dispose of human waste immediately. Clean yourself daily, focusing on your face, hands, feet, armpits, and groin.
3. Use solar ovens to cook food during sunny days; use a rocket stove otherwise. Heat water using a solar camp shower or a passive solar heater.
4. Use a wood stove, appropriate clothing, blankets, and sleeping bags to keep warm. Do nothing silly to stay warm or cook food like using an outdoor stove indoors or running a generator indoors (even if only partially enclosed).
5. Use battery-powered lanterns or solar lanterns; stockpile plenty of batteries, especially rechargeable options like Eneloop.
6. Determine what type of solar power setup works best for you (whole-house or something smaller), and if small-scale wind power is a viable option; reduce your power consumption, including making use of alternative ways to heat your home, cook food, and heat water.
7. Harden your home and security by banding with like-minded people and reading books on the topic (see book for details).

9 Additional Considerations

1. Children sometimes have special needs, such as diapers, formula or baby food, medications, educational supplies, and toys; be sure you have what they need.
2. Pets, too, need special food.
3. Pest control is more important than most people realize. Stockpile plenty of insecticides, rodent traps, and fly traps.

Keep your home clean inside and out, dispose of trash by burying or burning it, and quickly deal with problems when they arise rather than allow them to fester.
4. Don't barter, at least not initially, because it may encourage you to purchase items you'll never use instead of supplies you know you'll need at some point. It also places your safety at risk because you put yourself out there as somebody who has excess supplies.
5. Build relationships with people you can trust and rely upon; especially focus on people who bring their own supplies, skills, knowledge, and manpower to the table.
6. Learn to do with less or without, including rationing, finding effective alternatives (e.g., toilet paper alternatives), and deciding how important the daily supplies you use are. Make a list of things you use and then ensure you have plenty of the crucial items.
7. Reconsider unnecessary supplies and actions, like leaving the country, building an underground bunker, or prioritizing a bug out bag or retreat over your collapse survival plans.
8. Living in an apartment or condominium is less than ideal, but if you must, then build relationships and make plans now.
9. If you cannot financially afford to prepare, then you should put extra effort into searching for inexpensive survival items online, and take the time now to gain crucial knowledge and skills that will be of use post-collapse so that you can continue to afford the goods and services you expect.

The Most Important Reason We Choose to Prepare

1. Let's not forget about our children because they are the primary reason most of us preppers do what we do. Without a future for our children to inherit, it's difficult to

imagine any of this being worth doing. I, for one, firmly believe that preparing for collapse—whatever it looks like—is well worth doing for our children's sake.

Printed in Great Britain
by Amazon